P9-BZU-853

JACKIE KENNEDY: IMAGES AND REALITY

(A VOLUME IN THE PRESIDENTIAL WIVES SERIES)

OTHER BOOKS IN THE PRESIDENTIAL WIVES SERIES

DOLLEY MADISON
Paul M. Zall
2001. ISBN 1-56072-930-9. $34.

A "BULLY" FIRST LADY: EDITH KERMIT ROOSEVELT
Tom Lansford
2001. ISBN 1-59033-086-2.

SARAH CHILDRESS POLK, FIRST LADY OF TENNESSEE AND WASHINGTON
Barbara Bennett Peterson
2002. ISBN 1-59033-145-1.

FRANCES CLARA FOLSOM CLEVELAND
Stephen F. Robar
2002. ISBN 1-59033-245-8.

LUCRETIA
John Shaw
2002. ISBN 1-59033-349-7.

JACKIE KENNEDY: IMAGES AND REALITY

MOHAMMED BADRUL ALAM

Nova History Publications, Inc.
New York

Senior Editors: Susan Boriotti and Donna Dennis
Coordinating Editor: Tatiana Shohov
Office Manager: Annette Hellinger
Graphics: Wanda Serrano and Matt Dallow
Editorial Production: Maya Columbus, Alexandra Columbus, Alexis Klestov,
    Vladimir Klestov, Matthew Kozlowski and Lorna Loperfido
Circulation: Ave Maria Gonzalez, Vera Popovic, Luis Aviles, Sean Corkery,
    Raymond Davis, Melissa Diaz, Meagan Flaherty, Magdalena Nuñez,
    Marlene Nuñez, Jeannie Pappas and Frankie Punger
Communications and Acquisitions: Serge P Shohov
Marketing: Cathy DeGregory

Library of Congress Cataloging-in-Publication Data

Badrul Alam, Mohammed.
    Jackie Kennedy – images and reality / Mohammed Badrul Alam
        p cm. – (Presidential wives series)
    Includes bibliographical references and index.
    ISBN 1-59033-366-7.
        1. Onassis, Jacqueline Kennedy, 1929- 2. Celebrities—United States—Biography. 3.
Presidents' spouses—United States—Biography. I Title. II. Series.

CT275 O552 .B33 2002
973 922'092—dc21
[B]   2002026318

Copyright © 2004 by Nova History Publications, An Imprint of
    Nova Science Publishers, Inc
    400 Oser Ave, Suite 1600
    Hauppauge, New York 11788-3619
    Tele. 631-231-7269   Fax 631-231-8175
    e-mail: Novascience@earthlink.net
    Web Site: http://www novapublishers.com

Printed in the United States of America

CONTENTS

Foreword   vii
    Robert P. Watson

Preface   xi

Acknowledgements   xv

Chapter 1   Early Childhood and Youth   1

Chapter 2   Promising Start: Education and Career   5

Chapter 3   Marriage to John F. Kennedy   9

Chapter 4   Jackie During the
    White House Years, 1961-1963   29

Chapter 5   Jackie as Ambassador of Good Will   37

Chapter 6   Traumatic Days: Trip to Dallas and After   43

Chapter 7   Challenging Times: The Post-JFK Years   55

Chapter 8   Blossoming of a Greek Romance:
    Jackie's Marriage to Aristotle Onassis   61

Chapter 9   Back to New York: Post Onassis Years   65

Chapter 10   End of an American Icon   73

Bibliography   79

Index   85

FOREWORD

Robert P. Watson

The old saying that "behind every successful man is a woman" is perhaps nowhere more evident than in the White House. Even a cursory examination of the wives of presidents reveals a group of remarkable individuals who made many contributions to the lives and careers of their husbands, the presidency, and even the nation. Over the course of U.S. history first ladies have presided over state dinners, overseen extensive historical renovations of the Executive Mansion, held press conferences, campaigned for their husbands, testified before Congress, championed important social causes, and addressed the United Nations.

As a candidate for the presidency speaking of the role his wife would assume in his administration Bill Clinton stated that when the public elects a president, they are getting "two for the price of one!"

To an extent such a statement has always been true. First ladies have been a viable part of the presidency since the nation's founding. Of the men who served as president during the country's history, nearly all of them served with a first lady at their side. Only a handful of presidents have held the office without their spouses. For instance, both Andrew Jackson and Chester A. Arthur had lost their wives prior to their presidencies; Rachel Jackson dying in the interim between her husband's election and his inauguration and Ellen Arthur just prior to her husband's Vice Presidency. The wives of both Thomas Jefferson and Martin Van Buren passed away years before their presidencies. But they were exceptions. Only two bachelor presidents have been elected, Grover Cleveland and James Buchanan, however the former married while in office. Three presidential wives died while serving in the White House: Letitia Tyler, Caroline Harrison, and Ellen Wilson. However, both President John Tyler and President Woodrow Wilson later remarried while in office.

Presidential wives have served without pay and, until very recently, often without proper recognition. So too have they wielded political power and social influence despite the fact that they are neither elected nor appointed. In part because they are not elected or accountable to the citizenry and in part because of strict social conventions that precluded women from participating in politics for much of the nation's history, presidential wives have been forced to exercise their power and influence in a behind-the-scenes manner. Yet, in this capacity many wives have functioned as their husband's trusted confidante and private political advisor.

Presidential wives have faced great challenges, not the least of which include the loss of privacy and specter of assassination looming for themselves and their families. The presidency is arguably the most demanding job in the country and the challenges of the office are experienced by the president's family. Amazingly, several first ladies served while trying to raise a family. Presidential wives have faced severe scrutiny, an invasive press corps and curious public, and criticism from journalists and the president's political enemies. This is perhaps one of the experiences that all first ladies have shared. Not even popular wives like Martha Washington, Abigail Adams, or Jacqueline Kennedy were spared from harsh personal attacks.

The first ladyship has been the "unknown institution" of the White House. For most of its history it has been ignored by scholars and overlooked by those studying national and presidential politics. However, this is slowly changing. The public, press, and scholars are beginning to take note of the centrality of the first lady to the presidency. A new view of the president's spouse as a "partner" in the presidency is replacing more traditional views of presidential wives. Even though the Founding Fathers of the country gave no thought to the president's wife and the Constitution is silent concerning her duties, today the "office" has become a powerful, recognized institution within the presidency, complete with staff and budgetary resources that rival the so-called "key" presidential advisors.

It is also an intriguing office whose occupants are no less fascinating themselves. Indeed, the presidential wives are a diverse lot that includes new brides barely out of their teens to grandmothers who had spent a lifetime married to men that would become president. There have been women of refinement and wealth and there have been wives who would seem ill-prepared for the challenges of the White House. And of course, there have been successes and there have been failures.

The first ladyship is one of the nation's most challenging and dynamic public offices. So too is it an office still in development. In the words of First Lady Barbara Bush, concluding her remarks when delivering the commencement speech at Wellesley College, "And who knows? Somewhere out in this audience may even be someone who will one day follow in my footsteps, and preside over the White House as the President's spouse. I wish *him* well!"

In the volumes of this Series the reader will find the stories of women who fashioned the course of American history. It is the goal of the publishers and myself that this book and each volume in the Presidential Wives Series shed light on this important office and reveal the lives of the women behind the American presidency.

I hope you enjoy this book and the entire Series!

Robert P. Watson, Series Editor

PREFACE

The primary purpose of this book is to investigate the various facets of the life of Jacqueline Kennedy Onassis, a person who became an American icon for most of her adult life both before, during and after her years in the White House as the first lady of the United States. The book also examines the early years of Jacqueline Kennedy in order to find out whether there were any traits in her personality that prepared her for the more challenging times which she had to endure in her later years. The book makes an honest attempt to touch upon the fascinating life Jacqueline Kennedy led, which touched one and all across various spectrums of American society. The book covers Jackie's life from her early childhood years in East Hampton, Long Island to the final days in Manhattan, New York City.

Chapter One deals with Jackie's birth in July 28, 1929, as the first child to Janet Lee and John Bouvier II. This chapter also covers the childhood days of Jackie with her younger sister Lee, her love of horses and the way Jackie coped with the turbulent marital life of her parents and their eventual divorce.

Chapter Two looks at Jackie's educational career and the activities she was interested in from her kindergarten days on Long Island to her school days in Holton-Arms School in Washington, D.C., Porter's School in Farmington, Connecticut and her college years at Vassar College, the Sorbonne in Paris and George Washington University, from where she finally graduated in 1951.

Chapter Three focuses on Jackie's engagement and eventual marriage to John F. Kennedy, the junior Senator from the New England state of Massachusetts, and the way she earned everyone's heart and respect in the Kennedy family with her candor, sensitivity and single-minded devotion to her husband's welfare, both physical as well as political.

Chapter Four deals with Jacqueline Kennedy's role as the first lady of the United States from day one of the Kennedy presidency. In particular, the chapter shows Jackie's love for art and design during her White House years.

Chapter Five outlines Jackie's visit to Vienna and Paris with her husband, President John F. Kennedy and the way she charmed Soviet premier, Nikita Khruschev and French leader, Charles de Gaulle, respectively. The chapter also outlines Jackie's much publicized trip to India and Pakistan and how she earned the good will of the people of the Indian sub-continent through her personal diplomacy.

Chapter Six examines the pivotal moment of her life when she and President Kennedy made the momentous trip to Dallas, Texas on November 22, 1963. What happened in Dallas on November 22,

1963, and how history was created and what role Jackie played are the central focus of this chapter.

Chapter Seven elucidates the challenges Jackie faced in the aftermath of her husband's assassination and the way she coped with the loss by first sending a 'thank you' note to the new president, Lyndon B. Johnson, and by trying to make sure that the Kennedy legacy remained alive and well in the minds of the American public.

Chapter Eight highlights Jackie's life when she fell in love with a Greek shipping tycoon named Aristotle Onassis who she eventually married on Skorpios Island, Greece, on October 20, 1968. This chapter also describes how Jackie received a rather hostile reception from the American public who viewed the marriage as a betrayal of the 'Camelot' image that Jackie herself had played such a major role in creating.

Chapter Nine focuses on Jackie's life after the death of her second husband, Aristotle Onassis and how she picked up the pieces of her life once again and embarked upon a new career, this time as a book editor working at the Viking and Doubleday Publishing House in New York City.

Finally, Chapter Ten describes the final days of Jacqueline Kennedy's eventful life and career and how she raised her children, grandchildren and fought valiantly against lymphoma cancer.

ACKNOWLEDGEMENTS

This book has its origin from teaching a wide range of students in India, the USA and Japan. My students at Nimapara College (Utkal University, Bhubaneswar, India) were the early inspirations for sharpening my writing skills. Later in New Delhi where I earned my M.Phil degree in American Studies at Jawaharlal Nehru University, my professors, Dr. B.K. Shrivastava, Dr. M.S. Venkatramani and Dr. R.P. Kaushik taught me aspects of American popular culture and political institutions. My long stint working at the American Center Library in New Delhi opened up my eyes to the scope and breadth of literature on almost all important facets of American life.

In the United States, I attended Cornell University in Ithaca, New York, where I earned my M.A. and Ph.D. degrees in American Studies. While at Cornell, many professors instilled in me the various intricacies and complexities of political personalities and their spouses and their impact in the shaping of American society. Those professors are: Dr. Richard Polenberg, Dr. Mary Fainshod

Katzenstein, Dr. Milton Jacob Esman, Dr. Walter Lafeber, Dr. Martin Shefter, Dr. Benjamin Ginsburg, Dr. Peter Katzenstein, Dr. Richard Rosecrance, Dr. Ami Ayalon, Dr. Stewart Blumin, Dr. Joel Silbey, Dr. Myron Rush, Dr. George Kahin, Dr. Norman Uphoff, and Dr. Steven Jackson. At Cornell University Library, Mr. Ved Kayastha was of invaluable help in providing input and feedback whenever needed.

I am grateful to Dr. Bryan Reddick, Dean of Elmira College, New York, Dr. Anthony Layng, Professor of Anthropology, Dr. Robert Park, Professor of Political Science, Dr. Myra Glenn, Professor of History and Professor Peter Ladley, Department of English, all from the same institution, for encouraging me at all times. Dr. Frank Czerwinski of the State University of New York at Cortland offered me useful advice whenever I sought it. My colleagues at Midway College, Kentucky, namely, Dr. Robert Miller, Professor of Religion, Dr. Judith Hatchet, Professor of English, Dr. Glenna Graves, Professor of History, provided me with useful research assistance.

In Japan, where I have been teaching at Miyazaki International College in Southern Kyushu since January 1998, the following people helped shape my ideas and bring into focus the life and times of Jacqueline Kennedy. Among the colleagues who helped me are: Dr. Kate Greenfield, Dean; Dr. Getachew Felleke, Professor of Economics; Professor Jun Maeda, Professor of Japanese Literature; Dr. Daniel Bratton, Professor of English Literature; Dr. William Perry, Professor of English and Cross-Cultural Education; Dr. Scott Davis, Professor of Anthropology; Professor Mike Sagliano, Professor of English; Professor Katharine Isbell, Professor of English; Professor Amanda Bradley, Professor of English; Professor

Timothy Stewart, Professor of English; Professor Albert Evans, Professor of English; as well as faculty secretaries: Isuzu Stewart, Mayumi Okatomi and Kyoko Yamamoto. My students at the Miyazaki International College in the course, "North American Thought and Culture", provided interesting glimpses from the life of Jacqueline Kennedy as she shaped the American psyche for a number of decades beyond the 1960s. My friends working at other institutions in Japan also offered useful comments on this book project. Among those are: Dr. Joel Campbell (Professor of Political Science, Osaka University), Dr. Mika Mervioe (Professor of Political Science, University of Shimane), Dr. Jeffrey Folks (Professor of American Literature, Doshisa University at Kyoto), Dr. Dao Jiong Zha (Professor of Political Science, Niigata International University) and Professor Susan Tennant (Department of English, Nagoya University).

A special word of thanks to Dr. Robert P. Watson, Professor of Political Science at the Florida Atlantic University, who conceived the American First Wives Series project and in consultation with Nova Science Publishers, Hauppauge, New York, selected me to write a book on Jacqueline Bouvier Kennedy Onassis. Dr. Watson's constant prodding was a stimulating factor in my undertaking long hours in reading, researching, and writing the manuscript.

From the John F. Kennedy Presidential Library in Boston, Massachusetts, archivists, Mr. Allan Goodrich and Ms. Andrea Schoendube were of immense help in guiding my chapters and in providing me with necessary resource materials.

The greatest gratitude is owed to my mother, Mrs. Hedatun Nisa and brothers: Dr. Mohammed Shamsul Alam and Mohammed Aminul Alam, and sisters: Dr. (Mrs.) Swaleha Khatun, Mrs. Rahima

Khatun, Mrs. Sofia Khatun, my wife: Mrs. Gahartaj Rokeya and my children: Saira Alam, Zubair Alam, Sadaf Alam and Munawar Alam. Everyone allowed me the time and necessary emotional support I needed to complete my work. Much of my success is due to their love and affection at all times.

Dr. Mohammed Badrul Alam
Miyazaki, Japan

Chapter 1

EARLY CHILDHOOD AND YOUTH

Jack Bouvier was a tall, handsome man with good looks and a reputation for womanizing and wine. The son of an affluent lawyer, he was to attend the Ivy League institution, Yale University, located in New Haven, Connecticut. Bouvier was not particularly known for his academic brilliance. Rather, he spent his time on extra-curricular activities, romancing many women of his class, most of whom hailed from New York City. After graduating from Yale, he worked on Wall Street in a brokerage firm at his father's request. Bouvier made no positive impact on his family fortune while working on Wall Street.

Janet Lee was the eldest of three daughters of James T. Lee, President of the New York Central Savings Bank. Being a well-known celebrity in the social and political circles of New York, Jim Lee took his children to important social gatherings and parties. At one such party, Janet Lee met Bud Bouvier, Jack Bouvier's brother. Although Bud was an alcoholic and divorced, Janet was initially attracted to him. However, Bud's habitual dependency on alcohol made Janet change her mind and she set her sights on Bud's brother, Jack, who was more charming in any event. Finally, with parental consent, both Jack and Janet married on July 7, 1928, in a church in East Hampton, Long Island. Immediately thereafter, the couple left on a honeymoon trip to Europe aboard the ship *S. S. Aquitania.*

BIRTH OF JACKIE

The couple's first child, Jacqueline, was born on July 28, 1929, almost a year after the wedding. By this time, Jack "Black Jack" Bouvier was involved in several extra-marital affairs, much to the chagrin of Janet and her father, James T. Lee. Yet, Janet wanted to give the marriage a chance and encouraged Jack to concentrate on his profession (stock broker) in New York. Since Jack Bouvier did not have enough money of his own and whatever he had saved was lost due to bad investments and on his philandering habits, James Lee provided a rent-free apartment to Janet and Jack where they could stay with their newborn daughter, Jacqueline.

On March 3, 1933, the couple had a second daughter named Caroline Lee. Although Jack Bouvier had developed severe alcoholic habits by now, he still found some time to spend with his young daughters and their activities. Bouvier often took them to the playground and other outdoor jaunts such as picnics.

Jackie, being the eldest child, was sent to Chapin School for Girls in Manhattan for her early education. Even at that very tender age, she showed a fascination and proclivity for art, sculpture and horses.

Jack was still indulging in numerous affairs with other women and because of this, coupled with his alcoholic habits and consistent failure in his business dealings, Janet simply had enough and the couple began a trial separation for six months on September 30, 1936.

Jackie's mother, Janet, hoped that the trial separation would unite the couple in a more meaningful and mutual sense of understanding and would instill in Jack a sense of family responsibility. Since Jack refused to mend his ways and Janet was unwilling to cope with Jack's behavior any longer, Janet took the children to Reno, Nevada where she received a quickie divorce on June 6, 1940 on grounds of "extreme mental cruelty."

At the time of her parents' divorce, Jackie was eleven years old. Although Jackie was emotionally shattered by the divorce, she did not show it outwardly. Jackie loved both her mother and father very much. She was specially attached to her father. On the weekends when Jack was allowed visitation rights with the children whom he showered with gifts, he would take both Jackie and Lee and indulge them in such fun activities as camping and horseback riding. From her mother, Jackie developed the quality of self-assertiveness and a sense of confidence to move ahead in life in spite of adversity. However, Jackie, in the immediate aftermath of her parents' divorce, remained aloof from her close friends in school and spent a lot of time reading books.

Janet, meanwhile, was looking for alternative sources of physical and emotional support. After meeting and dating a number of men, she finally settled on a wealthy divorced man named Hugh Auchincloss and in June 1942 they married. Janet and Hugh had a total of five children from their union and from their previous marriages. Hugh Auchincloss owned large farms in Virginia Estate, Merrywood and Hammersmith Farm on Cape Cod. Jackie, being the eldest, helped take care of her siblings and also helped her mother and step-father in performing household chores.

Chapter 2

PROMISING START:
EDUCATION AND CAREER

In 1944, Jackie was enrolled at the famous Miss Porter's School in Farmington, Connecticut. The school was a boarding school where Jackie developed her independent streak of mind. Jackie graduated from Porter's School in June of 1947. Being a brilliant and a hard working student, Jackie won praise from all of her teachers and scored a perfect 'A' in all the subjects she took at the school. By this time, Jackie had also decided to make her own mark in life and 'not be a housewife,' restricted to what she believed would be a dull and unrewarding life of domestic labor.

At her formal "coming out" party that was held at Hugh's Hammersmith Farm in the presence of 300 guests, Jackie was named 'Debutante of the year.' After her high school graduation, Jackie enrolled at Vassar College in Poughkeepsie, New York, where she again excelled in all subjects and scored straight A's. In the summer of 1948, Jackie visited various European countries including England, France, Switzerland and Italy over a period of seven-weeks and gained valuable insights on the historical heritage and artistic splendor of those places. Jackie was simply fascinated by the grandeur of the ancient buildings and was keenly interested in the architectural design of these structures and their connection to European history.

LIFE AT SORBONNE

A year later, in August 1949, during her junior year abroad, Jackie went to France and joined the University of Paris, Sorbonne. It was at the Sorbonne that Jackie saw first-hand the rich history of French Civilization, including the Bastille around which modern French history was made on July 14, 1789. Jackie also mastered her fluency in the French language which helped her to gain a deep understanding of and appreciation for important works of French literature and history. Jackie also spent some time in Smith College in Massachusetts before enrolling at the George Washington University in Washington, D.C., where she earned a Bachelor of Arts degree with distinction and honors.

Immediately after her graduation from George Washington University, Jackie participated in a nationwide essay-writing competition sponsored by *Vogue* magazine. She came out ahead of 1,280 students and was awarded a free air ticket and all-expense paid trip to Paris.

Jackie's parents, particularly her step-father, Hugh Auchincloss, did not like the idea of Jackie accepting the *Vogue* trip and leaving the United States so soon again. Instead, Hugh offered Jackie and her younger sister, Lee, a free trip to Europe in the summer of 1951 on his behalf. On this trip, Jackie observed the historical sites surrounding the cities of Venice and Florence.

Upon her return from Europe, Jackie joined the *Washington Times-Herald* newspaper, as an inquiring reporter cum photographer. In this new job, Jackie performed a number of on-site reporting jobs in various locales in Washington, DC. She primarily visited houses and families taking pictures and preparing news items that were later published in the newspaper. What struck her colleagues and employees in the newspaper office was the dedication, seriousness and inquisitiveness with which Jackie performed her job. She accepted constructive criticism and was willing to learn from her fellow colleagues. With her good looks, superb team spirit and collegiality, Jackie earned everyone's attention by performing admirably at her job at the newspaper's office.

Chapter 3

MARRIAGE TO JOHN F. KENNEDY

Toward the end of 1952, while working at the *Washington Times-Herald*, Jackie was introduced to Congressman John F. Kennedy, a young Democrat from Massachusetts at a party at the house of Charles Bartlett. Although Jackie showed some interest in Jack, the relationship did not take off as might have been expected after their first encounter. Instead Jackie was more attracted to John Husted, a young, handsome investment banker with whom she was to become engaged.

KENNEDY AS A SENATOR

In November 1952, John F. Kennedy won a seat in the U.S. Senate from the state of Massachusetts in an impressive upset by unseating the popular Republican candidate, Henry Cabot Lodge, Jr.

With Jack in the U.S. Senate and Jackie's relationship with John Husted cooled off, Jackie and Jack met frequently. At a party hosted by the same Charles Bartlett, both Jack and Jackie began to think in terms of a possible long-term relationship. Since Jack was extremely busy with his senatorial duties and Jackie as a reporter - photographer at the *Washington Times-Herald*, they set the date of their wedding for September 12, 1953.

On January 20, 1953, at the second inaugural ceremony of President Dwight Eisenhower, Senator John F. Kennedy escorted Jackie to the President and the First Lady's inaugural ball. In 1953, Jackie was twenty-three and looked stunningly beautiful. Although Jack was very busy in the Senate, particularly in his committee assignment on the Committee on Government Operations, Jackie arranged a convenient date so that she could introduce Jack to her own father, "Black Jack" Bouvier who was residing in New York at the time. Finally, in February 1953, Jackie introduced Senator John F. Kennedy to her father at a restaurant in Manhattan. Jackie's father and Senator Kennedy developed a quick rapport and camaraderie, as both of them had similar opinions on subjects ranging from politics to social parties.

On April 18, 1953, Jackie's younger sister, Lee married Michael Canfield. Because Jackie had been very close to Lee since their childhood and both the sisters remained close, Jackie spent a great deal of time planning for her sister's wedding, making sure that all of the minute details were being taken care of.

At the end of May 1953, Jackie, on official assignment on behalf of the *Washington Herald-Times*, proceeded to London to cover the coronation ceremony of Queen Elizabeth II. Jackie wrote an insightful piece on this important news event which caught the attention of Jack Kennedy who sent Jackie a congratulatory message, "Article is excellent. Just you are missed. Love-Jack."[1]

By June, it became official that Jackie and Jack were going to marry in a few months time. In a news item that was published in *The New York Times* on June 25, 1953, it read,

> "Senator Kennedy to marry in fall, son of former envoy is fiancee of Miss Jacqueline Bouvier, Newport Society Girl."[2]

Senator Jack Kennedy also took Jackie to the Kennedy family compound in Massachusetts where he introduced her to his father, Ambassador Joe Kennedy, and his mother, Rose. Jackie impressed Joe with her easy demeanor and winsome smile. With Rose, Jackie quickly developed a friendly rapport. In the meantime, *Vogue* magazine published a full-page photo of Jackie with the caption, "a young woman of almost extravagant beauty"[3] amid the media hoopla and political attention on the September 1953 wedding of Senator Jack Kennedy to Jackie Bouvier.

PREPARATIONS FOR THE WEDDING

The pre-wedding parties commenced in earnest on September 2, 1953 with a bachelor's party that was held at the Parker House in Boston, where Jack, Jackie and the rest of the family members

---

[1] Donald Spoto, *Jacqueline Bouvier Kennedy Onassis: A Life*, New York: St. Martin's, 2000, p 108

[2] Ibid, p. 108

[3] Ibid, p. 108

welcomed friends, well wishers, Jack's campaign workers and his congressional staff members.

The wedding was held on September 12, 1953, at St. Mary's Church in Newport, Rhode Island in the presence of close friends and relatives. The nuptial ceremony was conducted by Archbishop (later Cardinal) Cushing of Boston. Jackie's younger sister, Lee, was Jackie's matron of honor and Bobby Kennedy was his older brother's best man.

Although Jackie preferred to have her father, Jack Bouvier, give her away in marriage, he was found completely drunk in a nearby hotel. Instead, Jackie's step father, Hugh Auchincloss, escorted the bride down the wedding aisle. The wedding reception at the Hammersmith Farm had some twelve hundred guests toasting the newly married couple. After spending two nights at the Waldorf Astoria Hotel in New York City, Jack and Jackie flew to the beach resort city of Acapulco, Mexico for their honeymoon.

BACK FROM THE HONEYMOON

Upon their return from Acapulco, Jackie went to Hyannisport where she met the large, extended Kennedy family. At first, she was uneasy at the sight of a big crowd of children and grandchildren at the Kennedy family home. But she soon endeared herself to the members of the Kennedy family, including Joe and Rose. While at the Kennedy residence, Jackie impressed her new relatives with her keen interest for works of art, classical music, literature and French antiques.

In the beginning of 1954, Jackie moved to Washington, D.C. to join Jack and assist him in his senatorial work. She spent long hours reading congressional records in order to get herself familiar with how the U.S. government operated. She also attended a congressional session when Jack was giving a speech in the floor of the U.S. Senate. In order to further her understanding of politics, Jackie enrolled in a course in American History at the School of Foreign Service at Georgetown University. During that time, Jackie also translated passages from the works of Jean Jacques Rousseau, Samuel Eliot Morrison, Henry Steele Comager, Voltaire and other noted writers. Being a voracious reader of the works of European philosophers during her college days, the translation job was highly satisfying to her.

JACK'S HEALTH PROBLEM

Around mid-1954, Jack's back problems surfaced again with crippling fury and he had to remain bedridden. Apart from the back pain, Jack was also experiencing the debilitating effects of Addison's disease. When he was admitted to New York Hospital for surgery on October 10, 1954, Jackie was at his bedside comforting him.

In spite of the doctor's best efforts, Jack's health continued to slide. On October 24, 1954, Jack's health deteriorated so fast that all hope for recovery had been abandoned. A priest was immediately summoned to administer the last rites to him. Jackie never left his side. She held Jack's hands and kept him informed of the headlines from the nation's leading newspapers. In order to keep Jack in good humor Jackie read movie reviews and jokes.

Surprisingly Jack began to show some signs of recovery, and his doctors permitted him to be discharged from the New York hospital and he was taken to the Kennedy family residence in Palm Beach, Florida. Jackie was also with Jack at Palm Beach looking after his needs and praying silently for Jack's recovery from the illness. Jack underwent a second operation on February 15, 1955 and Jackie, along with other family members, made sure that all possible arrangements and medical facilities be made available.

JACKIE AT JACK'S SIDE

During this seven month period of continuous hospitalization and recuperation, Jackie was very mindful of her husband's official tasks being discharged in his Washington Senate office. She kept Jack informed of all the major bills that were being presented in the U.S. Senate, including the progress of the bills in which Jack was particularly interested. Jackie was relaying information back and forth from Evelyn Lincoln, Jack's Washington-based secretary.

MAKING OF AN AWARD WINNING BOOK

While Jack was lying in the hospital, he conceived of the idea of writing a book. Soon the idea took the shape of a full-fledged writing project and the proposed book was titled, *Profiles in Courage*. Jackie contributed by taking notes for Jack and by giving the book focus and outlining major features of the book. She also worked with Theodore Sorensen and Jules Dowds as they prepared preliminary drafts of each chapter and showed them to Jack for his comments. When *Profiles in Courage*, was published in 1956. The book became an instant best seller all over the United States. The book was later adjudged as the best book in the biography category and was awarded the prestigious Pulitzer Prize.

Jackie was also instrumental in helping Kennedy to fine-tune how he presented his position on such important issues as the Nuclear Test Ban Treaty. With his wife's help, Kennedy successfully articulated how vital it was for the United States to have sign a treaty with the Soviet Union.

In the words of Arthur M. Schlesinger, Jr., "Jackie played a very interesting role in the development of Jack's thought." Schlesinger added, "She (Jackie) was not only interested in the longer issues, such as the human rights, she also quite enjoyed the nitty-gritty. She was amused by politicians fighting one day and appearing as close friends the next. On more serious matters, Jack could not read French and when it came to thinking about Vietnam, for example, he valued greatly her reactions and judgement about things."[4]

As a responsible wife dedicated to her husband's physical well being, Jackie continued to monitor his health and administer the requisite medicines at appropriate times as recommended by the physicians. What impressed the Kennedy family members was the calmness and patience in which Jackie undertook the strenuous task of taking care of Jack, who was continuously ill during the period of 1955 and 1956.

In October 1956, Jackie and Jack bought a home called Hickory Hill in McLean, Virginia, just off the Potomac river so as to be close to the Capitol Building in which Jack's Senate office was located. But the home also provided a degree of privacy, which the couple very much wanted.

---

[4] Ibid, p.125

THOUGHTS OF A 1956 PRESIDENTIAL RACE

Jack was very much interested in the idea of having a significant impact on the 1956 presidential race, as he felt that it was time for the United States to have a change in leadership after four years of the Republican Administration led by President Dwight Eisenhower. Although Jack had enormous respect for "Ike", he felt a victory by the Democratic Party in the 1956 election would be good for the country and provide the right direction for America's domestic and foreign policies.

Jackie fully supported her husband's intention to test the political waters during the 1956 presidential race. At the very least, Jack wanted to be the vice presidential running mate should Adlai Stevenson be the Democratic Party's presidential candidate in 1956.

Although Jackie was pregnant at this time, she managed to attend the Democratic Party Convention in which Jack formally endorsed Adlai Stevenson for president. Later, when Jack lost the key nominating battle for the vice presidential slot to Estes Kefauver, it was Jackie who counseled Jack to be supportive in defeat and work in a united manner for the victory of Stevenson-Kefauver in the November presidential election against the Republican ticket of Eisenhower-Nixon.

FIRST PERSONAL TRAGEDY FOR JACKIE

The first personal tragedy to hit Jackie and Jack occurred on August 23, 1956, when Jackie gave birth to a still-born child named *Arabella* at Newport, Rhode Island. Although it was a moment of profound personal sadness for her, she handled it calmly and with courage. Although Jack was at that time on a cruise in the Mediterranean Sea, Jackie never asked him to rush home. Upon Jack's return, both he and Jackie quietly celebrated their third marriage anniversary. They also made a decision to sell their newly purchased Hickory Hills residence to Bobby and Ethel Kennedy (Jack's younger brother and wife) who had several children by that time.

The year 1957 was an equally challenging year for Jackie. She preferred to stay indoors most of the time and kept herself busy by reading various books and magazines. On August 3, 1957, Jackie's father, "Black Jack" Bouvier, died in New York City. Being a divorcee leading a lonely life, Jack Bouvier had a difficult time in his life after his divorce from Janet, Jackie's mother. When Jackie learned of the demise of her father, with whom she was very sentimentally attached, she immediately flew to New York City along with Jack and personally supervised the funeral arrangements.

BIRTH OF CAROLINE

On November 27, 1957, on the eve of Thanksgiving Day, Jackie and Jack's daughter, Caroline Bouvier Kennedy, was born. It was a special moment for both the parents who thanked God for this bundle of joy. Archbishop Cushing baptized the newly-born daughter on December 13, 1957.

By the beginning of 1958, Jack was planning his 1958 Senate re-election campaign and a possible bid to enter the primaries for the 1960 presidential election. Jackie wholeheartedly gave her consent to Jack whenever he needed and even solicited appropriate persons and well wishers for political donations so vital for running a well-crafted re-election as well as a possible presidential bid. Jackie, however, was also aware that her privacy was being intruded upon because of the glare of publicity needed for a Senate and presidential campaign.

"Nothing disturbs me as much as interviews and journalists," Jack told her step-brother Yusha that year. "That's the trouble with a life in the public eye. I have always hated gossip-columnists, publicity about the private lives of public men. But if you make your living in public office, you're the property of every taxpaying citizen. Your whole life is an open book."[5]

Before the election day of 1958, Jackie was showing keen interest in all facets of the senatorial campaign of Jack Kennedy, who was standing for re-election from his home state of Massachusetts. According to Harvard economist and Kennedy friend John Kenneth Galbraith (and which was later corroborated by Arthur Schlesinger, Jr.), "Jackie was deeply involved with political decisions made by Jack. But she chose her own role carefully."[6]

Wherever Jack went, Jackie followed him in helping the organizers to draw a big crowd and often acting as a cheerleader at political rallies. Jackie's proficiency in various foreign languages also helped her in his presidential bid in garnering important votes for Jack from the influential ethnic communities living in various U.S. cities. Jackie was the kind of person who could excite the Italian immigrants in Boston by speaking in Italian, the Hispanic population of New York City by speaking in Spanish and speaking fluent French in cities of Louisiana.

---

[5] Bill Adler, ed; *The Unknown Wisdom of Jacqueline Kennedy Onassis*, New York: Citadel, 1994, p.74

[6] Arthur M. Schlesinger, Jr.; *A Thousand Days: John F. Kennedy in the White House*, Boston: Houghton Mifflin, 1965, p.17

JACK'S RE-ELECTION TO U.S. SENATE

On November 4, 1958, Jack Kennedy was re-elected to the U.S. Senate from the State of Massachusetts by a whopping 73.2 percent of the votes cast. Fresh from the electoral victory for the U.S. Senate, Jack and his advisors were charting a course for the next big electoral battle: to win the nomination for Jack from the Democratic Party for the presidency of the United States.

Jackie, meanwhile, was exhausted after appearing with Jack in the recent senatorial race which Jack won so resoundingly. Jackie went back to her favorite pastime of reading books written by such authors as Churchill, Prust, Colette, Kerouac, Coetean, Lamedussa, Memoirs of Casanova, etc. She also subscribed to *The Spectator, Connaissance des Arts, Realties, Vogue Paris and the London Times Literary Supplements*, in order to stay on top of the news for the art and literary sectors.

Jackie was also finding time to attend important social events such as her sister Lee's second marriage in March 1959 in a Virginia courthouse to a prince from London named Stanislas Radziwill. Both Jack and Jackie attended the reception. Afterwards, they met Winston Churchill at a private meeting along with Joe Kennedy, who was an ex-U.S. Ambassador to England.

CAMPAIGN IN WISCONSIN

By early 1960, Jack's presidential campaign was in full swing. Jackie accompanied Jack on a number of campaign stops all across the United States. On a scheduled trip to Wisconsin, which Jack could not attend as he had to rush to Washington, D.C. for a Senate vote, Jackie gladly filled in for her husband. She went from La Crosse to Stevens Point and on to other Wisconsin cities scouting for votes from across the state.

"You shake hundreds of hands in the afternoon and hundreds more at night," she said later. "You get so tired you catch yourself laughing and crying at the same time. But you pace yourself, and you get through it. You just look at it as something you have to do. You know it would come, and you knew it was worth it. The places blur after a while, they really do. I remember people, not places, in a receiving line. The thing you get from these people is a sense of shyness and anxiety and shinning expectancy. These women who come up to me at a meeting, they're as shy as I am. Sometimes, we just stand there smiling at each other and don't say anything ....."[7]

One important characteristic of Jackie's personality was never to denigrate anyone either in public or in private. This was reflected in the highly successful Wisconsin tour made by Jackie when she constantly refused to make any uncharitable comments about Hubert Humphrey, a fellow Democratic Party senator from the state of Minnesota, a neighboring state next to Wisconsin and who also happened to be a contender for the presidential nomination. Jackie's visit to Wisconsin was a high point of the campaign; as *The New York Times*, described it, under the headlines, "KENNEDY'S WIFE CHARMS VOTERS".

Jackie also had a penchant for humor to deflect potential thorny issues. Since Jack was a Catholic and many political commentators considered that to be a liability instead of an asset in a presidential race, Jackie commented, "I think it is unfair of people to be against

---

[7] Anthony Carl Sferrazza, *First Ladies. The Saga of the Presidents Wives*, New York: Morrow, 1991, p. 589

Jack because he's a Catholic. He's such a poor Catholic. Now, if it were Bobby, I could understand it."[8]

Choosing of LBJ as Jack's Running Mate

After a tireless campaign throughout the length and breadth of the country, when the Democratic Party Convention met in Los Angeles on July 14, 1960, Senator John F. Kennedy won the party's nomination for the post of the President of the United States.

In a deft political move, Jack chose Senate majority leader Lyndon B. Johnson of Texas as his running mate knowing fully well that a Texan would help the Democratic ticket in getting the crucial electoral votes from the Lone Star State.

Jackie, meanwhile, was pregnant and was resting at Cape Cod. When Jack informed her of his nomination as a presidential candidate of the Democratic Party and selection of LBJ as his running mate for the November election, Jackie was utterly thrilled.

Although she was at home waiting for the upcoming delivery of her child, Jackie wrote a syndicated newspaper column, "Campaign Wife" to energize the women voters of the country. Many people compared Jackie's style to that of another famous first lady, Eleanor Roosevelt who used to write "My Day" columns during her husband, Franklin D. Roosevelt's four presidential campaigns in 1932, 1936, 1940 and 1944. In her column, Jackie covered a wide range of topics from medical care for the elderly to educational funding by the federal government. Through careful use of the issues so central to the voter's mind, Jackie carved a niche for

---

[8] Ibid, Spoto, p.154

herself as it seemed the message she was delivering was coming from her heart and with a great deal of conviction.

On September 29, 1960, Jackie made her debut on the international scene when she appeared on the CBS TV Program, Person to Person, with her husband, Jack Kennedy. "What should be the major role of the First Lady?" asked host Charles Collingwood. "To take care of the President," replied Jackie, as if this were a silly question, "so he can best serve the people and not to fail her family, her husband and her children."[9]

HELPING JACK FOR THE PRESIDENTIAL DEBATE

Jackie also provided emotional and psychological support to Jack when he prepared for the soon-to-become famous televised debate with Vice President Richard Nixon, the Republican Party's candidate for the office of the President of the United States.

Although she was at an advanced state of her pregnancy, Jackie accompanied Jack to a ticker-tape parade in New York on October 19, barely two weeks before the election. More than a million people congregated on both sides of the road and caught a glimpse of Jackie, who could become the next First Lady of the United States. People from Lower Broadway North to Yonkers in Westchester county were delighted when Jackie waved her hand with a broad smile on her face.

In order to further cement Jack's support base among African-Americans, Jackie requested Harris Wofford, a lawyer with a special expertise on civil rights issues, to join the Kennedy team as

---

[9] Ibid, Spoto, p. 156

a speech writer and serve as a liaison between the campaign and the civil rights groups in various states.

When Civil Rights Leader, Dr. Martin Luther King, Jr., was arrested on October 19 in Atlanta while demonstrating at a luncheon counter, it was Jackie who called Mrs. Coretta Scott King and offered her moral support. Later, Bobby Kennedy, Jack's younger brother and member of the presidential campaign team, requested the sentencing judge release Dr. King without any delay.

ELECTION DAY JITTERS

As the election day approached, Jackie and the entire presidential campaign staff were restive as the opinion polls were unable to predict precisely who was ahead — Jack Kennedy or Richard Nixon. Although Jack seemed to be ahead in private polls in the crucial electorally-rich states such as New York, Illinois and Texas, the election outcome was by no means certain.

On election day, November 6, 1960, Jackie and Jack voted with the full expectation that Jack would win the race for the White House over Richard Nixon, who was Vice President under President Dwight Eisenhower for two terms, 1952-1960.

Some 68 million other Americans also voted in this momentous election which eventually turned out to be one of the closest presidential elections in America's political history. After they voted, both Jack and Jackie returned to their family residence at Hyannisport while their presidential campaign team waited at a nearby place with eyes fixed on the election results.

KENNEDY BEATS NIXON FOR THE
RACE TO THE WHITE HOUSE

After a roller coaster ride in which the election lead changed hands frequently between Nixon and Kennedy, only by the early hours of the next morning, did it known that John F. Kennedy had won the race and had been elected as the thirty-fifth President of the United States. Kennedy won 303 out of 537 electoral votes (including some of the big states), Kennedy also received 49.72 percent to Richard Nixon's 49.55 of the popular vote. As it turned out, Kennedy had barely squeaked by the popular vote benchmark by only 114,673 votes nationwide and in fact fewer than half of the states had voted for Jack Kennedy.

It was jubilation time in the Kennedy family as Joe threw a big party to celebrate his son's spectacular success in winning the most important elected public office in the world. It was a dream come true for most of the close knit Kennedy clan who had been planing for a Kennedy victory for many years.

Since Jackie was at a very advanced stage of her pregnancy, she preferred to stay away from the crowd and the partying that followed for many days at the Kennedy family compound in Hyannisport.

A RECORD FOR JFK

By winning the 1960 election for the White House, Jack Kennedy became the first Catholic ever to win this coveted race. Also, at age 46, he was the youngest person ever to be elected to the

Oval Office. He was also the first millionaire to be in the White House, having inherited a vast fortune from his father.

At age thirty-one, Jackie was at the height of her graceful beauty. Although she was not the youngest wife of an American President (that distinction went to the wives of Grover Cleveland and John Tyler), she (Jackie) was the first would-be-First Lady to be born in the 20th century. Jack also helped bring the glory back to the Democratic Party which had lost two consecutive elections to Republican Dwight Eisenhower. Jack wanted to herald the spirit of Democrats in an epoch making era of 1960 with a brand new team of advisors and cabinet officials.

JACKIE'S THOUGHTS ON MOVING TO THE WHITE HOUSE

Jackie, meanwhile, was contemplating the days and weeks ahead, particularly as to how she was going to raise her children in the White House amidst all the publicity and regalia attached to the office and mansion. Two days after the election, Jackie told Nan Robertson of *The New York Times* "I don't want my young children brought up by nurses and Secret Service men. I feel as though I have just turned into a piece of public property. It's really frightening to lose your anonymity at thirty-one."[10]

On Friday, November 11, two days after the election, and with the first round of victory parties and rallies over, Jack and Jackie along with their daughter Caroline left Cape Cod for Palm Beach, Florida. On the way, they stopped in Washington, D.C. briefly to

---

[10] Ibid, Spoto, p. 161. Also, see *The New York Times*, November 11, 1960

thank the well wishers and party activists who had worked tirelessly for the victory of the Kennedy-Johnson team in the 1960 election.

Upon arrival at the Kennedy family house in Palm Beach, Jackie summoned Letitia Baldridge from the White House staff and inquired about the rules, regulations and protocol matters surrounding White House receptions and dinners. Jackie, in particular, was interested to know about how previous first wives such as Mrs. Eisenhower, Mrs. Truman and Mrs. Roosevelt had interacted with the guests at gala receptions and dinners hosted by the White House.

BIRTH OF JOHN JUNIOR

On November 25, 1960, just days after Thanksgiving, Jackie gave birth to a six-pound baby boy named John F. Kennedy, Jr. News of the birth of a son to president-elect Kennedy and Jackie was splashed across all newspapers and media outlets in the US and abroad. It appeared as if a royal heir was born to a dynasty.

After staying in the hospital for two weeks, Jackie took her baby boy to a cathedral on N. Street in Washington where on December 9 he was christened. Later, Jackie, at the invitation of First Lady Mamie Eisenhower, took a two-hour tour of the White House, which was a custom between the outgoing administration and an incoming one.

JACKIE'S INITIAL IMPRESSIONS
OF THE WHITE HOUSE

At first sight of the White House, Jackie was unimpressed with what she saw. In the words of Jackie, "Oh, God. It's the worst place in the world! So cold and dreary - a dungeon like the Lubyanka (the Russian prison). It looks like it has been furnished by discount stores. I've never seen anything like it. I can't bear the thought of moving in! I hate it, hate it, hate it!" And to "Tish" Baldrige, Jackie confided that the place looked like a "hotel that has been decorated by a wholesale furniture store during a January clearance."[11]

Jackie was determined to maintain her sense of privacy, particularly for her children throughout the challenge of living in the residential quarters of the White House. Jackie's role model was Bess Truman who had been remarkably successful in raising her daughter, Margaret Truman, to her satisfaction in spite of living in the White House and, President Harry Truman being overwhelmingly busy during the historic events of World War II, the beginning of the Cold War and the onset of the Korean War. Jackie said, "She (Bess) brought her daughter to the White House at a most difficult age, and managed to keep her from being spoiled, so that she has made a happy marriage with a lovely child of her own. Mrs. Truman kept her family together in spite of White House demands, and that is the hardest thing to do."[12]

---

[11] Ibid, Adler, p. 46

[12] Marianne Means, *The Women in the White House*, New York; Random House, 1963, p. 269

Jackie instructed Tish Baldridge to make appropriate changes to the White House décor as well. "There are many things that can be done to make the White House warmer, more gracious, more distinguished,"[13] Jackie said. In particular, she was not happy the way Blue Room and Red Room were designed and wanted to do away with most of the paintings in these rooms as well as in other rooms of the White House that were used for official receptions and dinners for foreign dignitaries. Jackie wanted to bring a new look to suit her new taste. Her choice was to use a European and French architectural style.

At the time Jackie was giving instructions for a change in the White House's interior decoration, she was also assisting Jack to craft his inaugural speech, which was to be delivered immediately after the oath ceremony on January 20, 1961. Jackie lent her input and feedback as to what should be included in the Jack's vision of the 'New Frontier' that was to become a centerpiece of John F. Kennedy's new administration.

---

[13] Mary Van Rensselaer Thayer, *Jacqueline Kennedy: The White House Years,* Boston: Little, Brown, 1971, p. 11

Chapter 4

JACKIE DURING THE
WHITE HOUSE YEARS, 1961-1963

Immediately following John F. Kennedy's swearing in ceremony as president of the United States on January 20, 1961, Jackie moved from Blair House, where the Kennedy family members had been staying, to the White House at 1600 Pennsylvania Avenue.

One of the earliest decisions the couple made was to sell their old house at 3307 N Street in Washington, D.C., which Jack had bought as a senator after his marriage to Jackie. Luckily for both Jack and Jackie, they found a willing buyer who purchased their home for $110,000. The home had originally been bought in 1957 by the Kennedy's for $78,000.

Since Jackie always put a high premium on privacy, particularly for her children, she requested Bill Walton to locate a country retreat with enough space so that the couple's daughter,

Caroline, could have her horse-riding practice without the media intruding in to it. Ultimately, a site to the liking of Jackie and Jack was found at Glen Ora, which was a four-hundred acre estate near the town of Middleburg, Virginia and which was also within easy driving distance of Washington, D.C.

A GENERATIONAL CHANGE

Representing a new generation as she was only thirty-one and the third youngest first lady to reside in the White House, Jackie at the very outset in her official role as first lady of the United States insisted upon the latest designer fashions to satisfy her taste. She chose Oleg Cassini, a dress designer, to provide new wardrobes for her almost every week so that she could wear and showcase them at various state and other official functions.

Although Jackie was aware of the rumors of her husband's womanizing habits, she chose to ignore them as much as possible and put greater priority in fulfilling Jack's vision of starting a "New Frontier" in American society and in helping the President in all possible ways to fulfil his pledges to the American people. For Jackie, attending and working on Jack's physical and political well being were more paramount than his supposed infidelity.

Jackie was not particularly enamoured of the title of "First Lady". She told J. B. West, the White House Chief Usher, that she would prefer to be called simply Mrs. Kennedy, as the title 'First Lady' sounded like a saddle horse. Accordingly, the First Lady's staff members addressed Jackie as simply Mrs. Kennedy.

Since Jackie was a person of elegance and style with a deep passion for the arts, she ordered a massive restoration of the Executive Mansion in the White House. In fact, a good part of 1961 and 1962 was devoted to Jackie calling in various experts to make sure the White House (both interior as well as exterior) was refurbished and that the new "face lift" served both her taste and a sense of history.

Jackie and her staff made an inventory of all the furniture and furnishings from the past presidential families. They went to great lengths making sure that paintings and artifacts used were appropriate for each room in the private quarters and in official rooms. For the places where state dinners and receptions were held, Jackie took special care to hang on the wall only the most historic and important paintings of her choice.

As Jackie wanted to provide the White House a touch of history, she asked that antiques and the best of craftsmanship reflecting historic periods be used. She also wanted the White House renovation to reflect the new decade of 1960s along with the new Democratic Administration of John F. Kennedy, the youngest ever to be elected president of the United States.

Jackie was the first - ever first lady to organize a televised tour of the restored White House for the benefit of the press and the public. The media devoted extensive coverage to the newly restored White House rooms and the changing designs and décor as completed by Jackie. With the help of her staff members, Jackie also prepared a White House guide book which she edited, complete with photos and layouts of the important rooms in the private and official quarters of the Executive Mansion.

In Jackie's redecoration scheme, "Thomas Jefferson's inknede won its rightful place again in the White House. Van Buren's Empire Chairs reappeared, as did George Washington's armchair, Mrs. Grant's writing desk and China that had been chosen by Mr. Hayes, Mrs. Harrison and Mrs. Polk."[14]

TASTE FOR ALL THINGS FRENCH

Jackie took great care regarding the logistics of state dinners being hosted in the White House. One of the main changes was bringing in Ren Verdun as the White House's new French Chef. Perhaps this was to be expected, since Jackie had special affinities for French art, cuisine and culture due to her long years of association with France beginning in her college days.

Jackie soon became the nation's first unofficial minister of arts by changing the entire structure of White House reception and dinner galas. She wanted performing arts such as concerts and ballet to be added to the usual White House reception events for foreign dignitaries. Performers included violinist Alexander Schneider, Cellist Pablo Casals, violinist Isaac Stern, and composers such as Leonard Bernstein and Aaron Copland. Jackie also made a personal collection of the recordings of selected artists of her liking from Jazz, Latin American bossa nova and Chubby Checker along with hit albums such as the Beatles.

Jackie also had a preference for movies from Europe to be screened at the White House dinners. It included films by François

---

[14] Ibid, Spoto, p.176

Truffaut (Jules et Jim), Alain Resnais (L'annee Derniere a Marienbad), and Federico Fellini (La Dolce Vita).

Jackie instructed her staff to add "to the Vice President of the United States and Mrs. Johnson"; at the end of "Hail to the Chief" the song that was usually played at state and ceremonial visits when both the President and the First Lady were in attendance.

Ever since John F. Kennedy was elected in the 1960 presidential election, Jackie was mindful of the significant support Jack received by choosing Lyndon B. Johnson as his vice presidential running mate from the electorally rich state of Texas. Mr. Johnson, a seasoned politician of high stature with a long career as a powerful U.S. Senator from Texas and as Senate Majority Leader, provided wise counsel to the new president and his administration. President Kennedy wanted to cultivate and nurture that relationship with the Vice President and his wife and made them feel welcome to the White House at all official and state functions.

Jackie never once boasted that she held a privileged position as First Lady at the White House. She did not want anyone to feel intimidated. For Jackie, the White House was like a house taken on rent and she was there as a custodian on a temporary basis.

By early 1963, Jackie was pregnant again. In June, the President traveled to Colorado, California, Texas and Hawaii, and then on to Germany, Ireland, England and Italy without Jackie. The First Lady preferred to stay at home waiting for the baby's delivery.

PATRICK'S DEATH

On July 24, 1963, Jack and Jackie spent the day quietly at the family residence celebrating Jackie's thirty-four birthday. Shortly thereafter, on August 7, 1963, Jackie delivered, by Cesarean section, a four pound son, named, Patrick Bouvier Kennedy, who was born six weeks premature. Patrick had serious breathing and other complications at the time of his birth. In spite of the best efforts made by the doctors, they could not save his life and, within forty-eight hours, Patrick died. Their son's death brought Jack and Jackie closer than ever as they sought inner strength from each other's companionship. It also affected their relationship profoundly and both of them became much more attentive to each other's emotional needs and support.

Still grieving and in need of a change of scene and distraction, on October 1, 1963, Jackie along with Under Secretary of Commerce, Franklin D. Roosevelt, Jr. and his wife, flew from New York to the port of Piraeus. There they boarded the Christina for few days of rest and relaxation in the company of Jackie's sister, Lee and her husband.

Jackie returned to Washington, D.C. on October 12, 1963 in order to get herself and the President ready for the important trip to Dallas, Texas. Jackie was in attendance at the meetings where details of the Texas trip were being discussed, including where the couple would stay, which cities to visit, which receptions to attend and which clothes to wear. As if this was Jackie's rendezvous with destiny, Jackie seemed to pay more attention to all the "nitty gritty" details for the Texas trip, perhaps knowing her husband's interest in using the event as part of his pre-campaign for the 1964 presidential race was fast approaching. Texas, as was the case in the 1960 election, could again play a crucial role in Kennedy's re-election.

Chapter 5

JACKIE AS AMBASSADOR OF GOOD WILL

Jacqueline Kennedy Onassis had spent quite a number of years during her school and college days traveling and studying in Europe, particularly at the Sorbonne in France and showed great skills in mastering international diplomacy during her husband's presidency.

She was a constant source of inspiration to President John F. Kennedy during the historic moments of his presidency such as the erection of the Berlin Wall, the Bay of Pigs incident and the Cuban Missile Crisis. Jackie was an influential figure in shaping the Kennedy Doctrine for nuclear disarmament at a time when the Soviet Union was competing with the United States for global dominance in the ideological arena and in increasing its own sphere of influence. On numerous occasions, Jackie made inquiries of Deputy Secretary of State, Roswell Gilpatric, on the functioning of the Pentagon and whether funding for the agency was adequate or not. On the eve of the official state visit of King Hassan of Morocco to the United States, Jackie wrote a personal letter five pages long to him highlighting the importance the Kennedy Administration attached to the bilateral relationship between Morocco and the United States and how it was in the U.S. interest to have stable regimes in the North African region.

In the Spring of 1961, just a few months into the Kennedy presidency, Jackie joined the President on official trips to Canada, France and Austria. In her meeting with Canadian Prime Minister, John Diefenbaker in May 1961, she charmed him with her vast knowledge of the history and geography of Canada, a nation important to the United States and a strategic ally of NATO.

TRIP TO PARIS

Perhaps the crowning moment of this trip was her visit to Paris, a place quite familiar to Jackie since her school days at the Sorbonne and her fascination with French history and architecture. Wherever Jackie visited in Paris during those four days, from May 31 to June 3, 1961, she was cheered wildly with the shouts of "Vive Jacques." Jackie impressed French President Charles de Gaulle at the official banquet held in her husband's honor with fluent and splendid oratory in French. So successful was the First Lady's visit to France that Jack Kennedy described himself as the man who accompanied Jacqueline Kennedy to Paris which was meant as a tribute to the First Lady's enormous popularity with the masses in Paris.

In Vienna, while Kennedy was busy discussing matters of state with Soviet Premier Nikita Khruschev, it was Jackie Kennedy who stole the limelight with her personal wit and unflappable charm. Later in that trip she met Queen Elizabeth II at Buckingham Palace, London, for a personal audience with the Queen. The news of this meeting made headlines in all the major British and European newspapers.

In the latter part of 1961, Jackie visited Puerto Rico, Venezuela and Columbia. Because of Jackie's near native fluency in Spanish, it was easy for her to communicate to the crowd wherever she visited during her Latin American tour. Jackie's success in being an effective communicator earned a tremendous amount of good will towards her and for the United States.

VISIT TO INDIA

Another historic trip that Jackie made while she was the first lady was to India and Pakistan in 1962. Ever since Kennedy's victory in the 1960 presidential election and the nomination and appointment of family friend and famed Harvard economist, John Kenneth Galbraith, as the new U.S. Ambassador to India, Jackie had been planning a trip to India. She was fascinated with India which once was the 'Jewel in the Crown' of the British empire. Jackie's tentative preparation for the tour went awry when in December 20, 1961, when India took military action in the remaining Portuguese territory of Goa in Western India.

However, Jackie was determined to make this visit as she wanted to see India, a land with immense diversities and contrasts and a rare democracy among third world nations that had achieved independence from Great Britain in 1947, after two hundred years of colonial rule.

Along with her sister, Lee, Jackie and her presidential team (aides, speech writers, personal attendants, reporters, photographers, Secret Service Agents, etc) arrived in India on March 12, 1962. Jackie Kennedy was hailed by various commentators who covered her visit as the mystical Durga, the Goddess of Power in Hindu dominated India. Jackie, as part of her official duties in New Delhi, the nation's capital, met President Dr. S. Radhakrishnan, Prime Minister Jawaharlal Nehru and his daughter Mrs. Indira Gandhi who was fast emerging as a politician in her own right. Jackie placed a wreath at the Rajghat grave site of Mohandas K. Gandhi, the founder of modern India. Later, the First Lady visited the city of Agra and the historic Taj Mahal, one of the seven man-made wonders of the modern world. She also visited the holy city of Benares where Hindu pilgrims bathed in the Ganges river to wash away their sins in order to attain Nirvana. Jackie and her entourage also visited Fathepur Sikri, where they delighted in seeing the ancient forts of the Mughal period that ruled over India in the sixteenth and seventeenth centuries. They also visited other central Indian desert cities of Jaipur and Udaipur meeting old Maharajas (kings) symbolizing India's imperial past.

Jackie's trip to India had a positive impact on her Indian hosts as well as upon herself. She was completely captivated at the artistic splendor she encountered and the richness of the culture of India. "Jackie's effect on the Indians was just wonderful,"[15] Galbraith remembered (and), she developed her interest in Indian art and

---

[15] Sarah Bradford, *America's Queen· The Life of Jacqueline Kennedy Onassis*, New York: Viking, 2000, p.218

architecture ...(and her) visit was the high spot of India-American relations. Nehru was by all odds, the strongest figure in India and he was captured by Jacqueline Kennedy."[16] Mrs. Kitty Galbraith remembered the close personal, chemistry between Prime Minister Nehru and the First Lady, Jackie. "I watched Jackie and Nehru sitting on the steps and they were laughing together and he had his white jacket with a red rose on it and she had worn a red and white dress ... and they were acting like school children. They were just talking back and forth and laughing."[17] "I think Nehru was particularly delighted to be the host for an American who did not feel obliged to talk about politics at every suitable moment and was so obviously interested in Indian art."[18] Galbraith said. Asked if Jackie's visit had a helpful effect on India-American relations, Galbraith replied, "Oh, sure. It established Nehru as I said. India had a strong government at that time and the epitome of strength was Nehru. (He) was greatly attracted by Jackie, and this led to a more amiable view of the United States without much doubt."[19]

From her triumphant trip to India, Jackie and her entourage went to Pakistan where they were state guests of Field Marshall Ayub Khan, President of Pakistan. Jackie witnessed a horse show featuring dancing horses, camels swaying their bodies to the tune of rock and roll and other curious and entertaining performances during her brief visit to Pakistan. Jackie also found some time to visit the historic Shalimar Bagh, a garden created by Mughal emperor Shah Jahan in the mid-seventeenth century in the city of Lahore and also the historic trade route known as the Khyber Pass

---

[16] Ibid, p.218
[17] Ibid, p.218
[18] Ibid, p.218
[19] Ibid, p.218

through which many invaders had come to the Indian sub-continent. In Pakistan's press, Jackie was named as "Ameriki Rani" (Queen of America) through her regal touch and easy and affable demeanor.

Even after ceasing to be America's First Lady following Kennedy's death, Jackie still made a number of foreign trips. In October 1967, Jackie and David Harlech, trustee of the Kennedy School of Government, visited Cambodia and Thailand. In Cambodia, she spoke to Prince Norodam Sihanouk while demonstrating her clout and international popularity. Her visit helped in soothing anti-American feelings which were on the ascendance due to increased US military activity in adjoining areas of Vietnam and Indo-China.

In the later years of her life, Jackie also made some foreign trips including her visit to China in 1979 with I. M. Pei and his wife, Eileen, and New York's socialites such as Marietta Tree, Evangelina Bruce, and Bunny Mellon. With friends Cary and Edith Welch, Jackie made two extensive trips back to India, one to the northern part in January 1984 and the other to the Southern landscape of India in January 1989. In particular, Jackie was interested in India's temple architecture and her knowledge on this subject helped her prepare a catalog for an exhibition at New York's Metropolitan Museum of Art, entitled, "Indian Art and Culture, 1300 to 1900."

Chapter 6

TRAUMATIC DAYS:
TRIP TO DALLAS AND AFTER

Although on numerous occasions Jackie had participated in her husband's senatorial and presidential campaigns, she had not made any official political appearances alongside her husband until their trip to Dallas, Texas, on November 22, 1963.

During the planning of the trip to Texas, President Kennedy was aware of the personal feud between his Vice President, Lyndon B. Johnson, and Senator Ralph Yarborough, the senior senator from Texas who were competing for increased political influence in the lone star state. Both Johnson and Yarborough were also worried about protests from Texans opposed to President Kennedy.

IMPORTANCE OF TEXAS

Texas was extremely important to President Kennedy, particularly as the state had a rich electoral college vote. In a close presidential contest such as in 1960, it (the state of Texas) tipped the balance in favor of the Kennedy-Johnson team over Nixon-Cabot Lodge. One of the prime reasons why Kennedy chose LBJ as his running mate in 1960 was in fact the importance of Texas in a presidential campaign, as Johnson was a popular and powerful politician in Texas. The choice might also have influenced the voters of the neighboring states around Texas, as LBJ had the ability to carry Texas by himself for the Democratic ticket.

By the autumn of 1963, President Kennedy was contemplating reelection in 1964. He very much wanted to sooth the frayed tempers of the political "bigwigs" of the state of Texas. He needed them to work unitedly and cohesively for a big win in the 1964 election. There was speculation that Governor John Connally was not in good terms with Vice President Lyndon Johnson, and President Kennedy made it a point to meet one-on-one with the powerful Governor of Texas in order to cement the base of the Democratic Party in that state and also to energize grassroots workers.

In order to woo the public in this important trip to Texas, the President wanted the First Lady to be eloquent in her best dress. That dress was personally selected by the President. She wore her pink suit and pill-box hat.

Along with their entourage, the President and the First Lady left Andrews Air Force Base just outside Washington, D.C. on November 22, 1963 and arrived in San Antonio a few hours later.

After short stops in Austin and Fort Worth, the President and the First Lady flew to Dallas.

It was a sunny day in Dallas and a huge, enthusiastic crowd waiting for them at the Dallas Airport where a small girl presented the First Lady with a bouquet of red roses. The President and the First Lady were in a cheerful mood waving at the crowd. After the initial airport reception and protocol was over, the Governor and his wife, Mrs. Connally, escorted President Kennedy and Mrs. Kennedy in an open limousine and presidential motorcade. Vice President Lyndon Johnson and his wife, Lady Bird, were in another car. They were followed by a number of Secret Service personnel and Texas state troopers who were in other cars preceding and also following the convoy including the presidential limousine. President Kennedy was sitting in the back of the car on the right side while Jackie was sitting beside her husband to the left. Governor and Mrs. Connally were in the 'jump' seats, in front of them. Looking at the thunderous applause from the large crowd who had assembled on that picturesque day in Dallas, Mrs. Connally said, "Mr. President, you certainly cannot say that Dallas does not love you."[20]

As the presidential motorcade approached the Texas Book Depository and making a turn, suddenly there were burst of loud noises. At first, some people believed they were fire crackers celebrating the arrival of President and Mrs. Kennedy to the city. It turned out to be three blasts from a rifle.

In her deposition before the Warren Commission in 1964, Jackie Kennedy said, "All I remember was seeing my husband. He had this sort of quizzical look on his face, and his hand went up —

---

[20] Ibid, Spoto, p.200. Also, see, Michael Beschloss, "An Assassination Diary," *Newsweek*, November 23, 1998

it must have been his left hand."[21] The first bullet had entered the back of John Kennedy's back and pierced through the front of his throat. The second bullet to hit the President entered the back of his head and exploded on impact on the right side of it. All Jackie could remember was pools of blood, broken tissues from the President's skull and some flesh. "I turned and looked at him. I could see a piece of skull lying on my lap and I remember it was flesh colored. I remember thinking he just looked as if he had a slight headache."[22]

In the car, there were pieces of bone, brain tissue and bits of his reddish hair flying all over. When Jackie crawled to the trunk of the car to retrieve a chunk of Jack's skull, she was pushed back to her seat by Secret Service agent Clint Hill. Mr. Hill, by this time, had managed to jump on the presidential limousine with the apprehension that further attacks on the President were probably underway. Upon seeing Clint Hill, Jackie screamed, "They have killed my husband. I have his brains in my hands."[23]

In her deposition before the Warren Commission, Jackie said, "I just remember falling on him and saying, 'Oh, no, no, no, no, oh, my God, they have shot my husband. I was shaking. And just being down in the car with his head in my lap. And it just seemed an eternity."[24]

The presidential motorcade sped towards the nearby Parkland Hospital and was taken through an emergency exit. With presidential assistants, Dave Powers, Kenneth O'Donnell and others,

---

[21] *The New York Times*, November 23, 1964

[22] Ibid

[23] Kenneth O' Donnell and David F. Powers, *Memoirs of John F. Kennedy*, Boston: Little, Brown and Company, 1972, p.27-28

[24] Lawrence K. Altman, "Doctors Affirm Kennedy Autopsy Report," *The New York Times*, May 20, 1992. Also, see Ibid, Spoto, p.222

Jackie helped them in lifting the President's body to a stretcher. In spite of the valiant efforts of the doctors who were attending the President, all was in vain. The President was administered last rites by a local priest who had to be rushed to the hospital for the service. Jackie was standing nearby, completely dazed and shocked at the sudden turn of events unfolding right in front of her eyes. Jackie quietly slipped off her wedding ring and gently put it on Jack's finger. It was just after twelve-thirty. John F. Kennedy, the thirty-fifth President of the United States, was pronounced dead. He had been in office for just two years, ten months, and two days, and died at the age of forty-six.

Air Force One, which had so recently taken President Kennedy on the trip to Dallas, was now on its return trip back to Washington with the dead President in its cabin. On board now was also the new President, Lyndon B. Johnson who, as per the U.S. Constitution, took over as Chief Executive by taking the oath of office inside the airborne flight. It was a poignant moment when Jacqueline Kennedy, in spite of being grief stricken, chose to attend the swearing in ceremony of Lyndon B. Johnson as the next President of the United States. Even though the new first lady, Lady Bird, requested Jackie to change her clothes, the latter insisted on wearing the same clothes she had worn earlier while she was with Jack Kennedy inside the presidential motorcade, with stains of blood distinctly visible.

Air Force One touched down at Andrews Air Force Base in Maryland on Saturday, November 23. Upon the plane's arrival, JFK's body was lowered to an ambulance and Jackie, escorted by Attorney General Robert Kennedy (the slain President's younger brother), and other family members, relatives, and presidential staff from the White House, went to Bethesda Naval Hospital where an autopsy was performed. Later, Kennedy's body was taken to the White House where Jackie and her two children, Caroline and John, Jr., as well as relatives from both sides of the family offered prayers in silence.

THE SOLEMN SCENE

On Sunday, November 24, President Kennedy's body was taken to the Capitol Rotunda where it was wrapped in the U.S. flag. Jackie visited her husband's coffin several times during the day, shuttling between the White House and the Capitol Building. Members of both the Senate and the House of Representatives, state governors, and other dignitaries and foreign leaders also paid their last respects to the slain president. For the American people sitting at home in their living rooms or at their places of work, all eyes were glued to the TV networks, which were providing LIVE coverage of every moment of JFK's funeral ceremony including the highly moving scene of John Kennedy Junior's salute to his slain father. The people were touched at Jackie's simple demeanor in this, the saddest moment of her life.

The same day that Kennedy's body was honored in the Capitol Rotunda, another drama was being enacted in a Dallas court room. There, a night club owner, Jack Ruby, assassinated Lee Harvey Oswald at point-blank range from his revolver. The police believed Oswald was the person who fatally shot the President and wounded Governor Connally. Oswald would never be brought to trial.

Meanwhile, Jackie was sharing her grief and inner thoughts with Kennedy family members, in particular, Attorney General

Bobby Kennedy, who was very close to his older brother and Senator Teddy Kennedy, the youngest of the Kennedy brothers.

On Monday, November 25, in the presence of world dignitaries and leaders from around the nation as well as ordinary people from all walks of life, Kennedy's coffin that was carried by a horse-drawn carriage and was preceded by a riderless horse. He was buried in Arlington National cemetery near the Potomac river. The eternal flame was lit.

Through all these traumatic days, Jackie never for a moment lost her public composure. Jackie even instructed her aides, J.B. West and Pierre Salinger to have John, Jr.'s birthday celebrated in the usual way even though it coincided tragically with the day when President Kennedy was buried. Similarly, Jackie along with her close associates, also celebrated daughter Caroline's birthday two days later.

In the reception that was held after the burial ceremony, the foreign dignitaries including presidents, prime ministers, and kings from many nations, assembled at the White House. Jackie Kennedy personally thanked them for taking time off on short notice and flying to Washington, D.C. from far away places in order to pay respects to the late President.

Now that she was no longer the first lady, the problem for Jackie was more immediate in terms of housing and the need for continuous financial support to maintain herself and her two children, Caroline and John, Jr. Congress quickly approved a measure to provide Jackie with a $50,000 budget, two years of staff assistance, free mailing privileges, and a year of Secret Service protection. There were also numerous people who volunteered to answer the thousands of letters of mail Jackie received each day from practically every part of the world. Congress put this financial package for Jackie in a fast track as there was no precedent for helping a widow of a slain President to fulfil her basic financial and other legitimate needs. Under the existing law at that time, Jackie was only entitled to a widow's pension of $10,000 annually for life or until she remarried.

Jackie also wrote a personal letter to the new President, Lyndon B. Johnson, thanking him for his extraordinary kindness and sense of empathy shown to her and her children, Caroline and John, Jr. during the crisis. It read:

> "Dear Mr. President ,
> Thank you for walking yesterday – behind Jack. You did not have to do that – I am sure many people forbid you to take such a risk, but you did it anyway.
>
> Thank you for your letters, to my children. What those letters will mean to them later-you can imagine. The touching thing is, they have always loved you so much, they were most moved to have a letter from you now.
>
> And most of all, Mr. President, thank you for the way you have always treated me – the way you and Lady Bird have always been to me – before, when Jack was alive, and now as President.
>
> I think the relationship of the Presidential and Vice Presidential families could be rather a strained one. For the history I have been reading ever since I came to the White House, I gather it often was in the past.

But you were Jack's right arm – and I always thought the greatest act of a gentleman that I had seen on this earth was how you – the Majority Leader when he came to the Senate as just another little freshman who looked up to you and took orders from you – could then serve as Vice President to a man who had served under you and been taught by you.

But more than that we were friends, all four of us. All you did for me was as a friend and the happy times we had, I always thought, way before the nomination, that Lady Bird should be the First Lady – but I don't need to tell you here what I think of her qualities – her extraordinary grace of character – her willingness to assume every burden. She assumed so many for me and I love her very much. And I love your two daughters – Lynda Bird most because I know her the best – and we first met when neither of us could get a seat to hear President Eisenhower's State of the Union Message and someone found us a place on one of the steps in the aisle where we sat together. If we had known then what our relationship would be now.

...Late last night, a moving man asked me if I wanted Jack's ship pictures left on the wall (of the Oval office) for you (they were clearing the office to make room for you) I said, 'No', because I remembered all the fun Jack those first days hanging the pictures of things he loved, setting out his collection of whale's teeth, etc.

But, of course, they are there only waiting for you to ask for them if the walls look too bare. I thought you would want to put things from Texas on it – I

pictured some – long hours – I hope you put them
somewhere.

It cannot be very much help to your first day in office
to hear children on the lawn at recess. It is just one
more example of your kindness that you let them stay
– I promise thy will soon be gone.

Thank you, Mr. President.
Respectfully,
Jackie"[25]

Jackie was grateful to the Johnsons for giving permission for
use of the White House residential quarters for a reasonable length
of time. Jackie was also deeply appreciative of the new First Lady's
affectionate behavior and genuine concern in making sure that the
staff members of the new administration continued to be of help to
Jackie in all possible ways.

Although Jackie was immersed in thought about her future, she
was also extremely possessive about her desire to keep the Kennedy
legacy alive. With steadfast determination, Jackie invited historian
Theodore Sorensen to her residence on November 29, 1963 in order
to make sure that the public remembered 'Camelot', the thousand
days of the Kennedy presidency, in a positive light.

Jackie was also making plans to move out of the White House.
A number of friends were helping her stay out of the limelight.
Finally, on December 6, 1963, with the help of Professor John
Kenneth Galbraith, a long time Kennedy family friend and U.S.

---

[25] Merle Miller, *Lyndon: An Oral Biography*, New York: Putnam's, 1980, p. 335-336

Ambassador to India, Jackie and the children moved from the White House to the home of Averall Harriman, under-Secretary of State and a Democratic Party activist. The family settled down in the Georgetown section of Washington, D.C.

As soon as Jackie moved to Georgetown, it became the hub of political activity for Democrats. The American public remained quite interested in what role Jackie would play in society in the immediate aftermath of her husband's assassination. Jackie's life in Georgetown was made easier by frequent visits to her home from Kennedy family members, particularly Bobby Kennedy, his wife Ethel, and their children who spent many long hours with Jackie, Caroline, and John, Jr. These visits helped Jackie ease the painful ordeal and the psychological shock she had to endure since the dreadful day in Dallas, Texas. Caroline and John, Jr., also liked Georgetown as they could continue their day-care schooling and by staying in a city which had become a part of their early life during their father's presidency and congressional days.

Chapter 7

CHALLENGING TIMES:
THE POST-JFK YEARS

John F. Kennedy's assassination in Dallas was a bolt from the blue for Jackie and it took her quite some time to even partially recover from the psychological trauma. She was also saddled with raising two very young children and providing them for their complete physical and emotional support along with making arrangement for their education and overall welfare. At this time of distress, Kennedy family members, along with a large group of Kennedy friends and advisors, and even ordinary people whose lives were touched by John F. Kennedy, came forward to offer their unstinted help and solace to the family in every possible way.

Mindful of the tasks set out by the new president, Lyndon B. Johnson, and his desire to put his team in place in the White House, Jackie and her children had left the White House residential quarters on December 6, 1963. Although Jackie was in good terms with LBJ and his wife, and in spite of President Johnson's offer to Jackie to maintain a small White House office and continue her public relations activities, Jackie decided to move completely out of the residential quarters of the White House. Her new home at Averall Harriman's house in the Georgetown section of Washington, D.C. became the new hub of social and political activities.

In January 1964, Jackie thanked the American people for the love, affection and advice shown to her and the children. She was moved by these gestures and it helped Jackie to cope with the loss of her husband. A month later in February, Jackie made a trip to New York City and, in consultation with her family members and friends, bought a 15-room apartment on Fifth Avenue. As Jackie had a flair for style and artistic tastes, she spent an additional $124,000 on redecoration. Since Jackie put a premium on privacy, the new house in New York was strategically located away from the glaring eyes of the media and inquisitive onlookers. She also wanted to be out of Washington in order to start a new phase of her life away from the painful episodes of her husband's assassination, funeral, and the haunting memories surrounding those solemn events.

Soon after moving to New York, Jackie was busy riding a horse in a nearby New Jersey derby. It had been one of her favorite activities ever since she won numerous trophies in various horse races at a very young age.

In 1967, accompanied by Lord Harlech, Jackie made a low profile visit to war-torn Cambodia to meet Prince Sihanouk. Jackie acted as America's unofficial good will ambassador in toning down the anti-American sentiments that were sweeping Cambodia in light of America's ongoing engagement in Vietnam and Indo-China at that time.

Jackie, although maintaining public neutrality on her own possible political leanings, was very supportive of Bobby Kennedy's bid for the 1968 presidential election.

SUPPORT FOR BOBBY'S PRESIDENTIAL BID

Ever since Jackie married Jack and moved to Massachusetts, she could clearly see Robert (Bobby) Kennedy as a rising star who had the communicative skills and political savvy needed in order to get elected in to the highest office in the United States. That Robert Kennedy was elected from the politically important state of New York as a Senator and that he accomplished this away from the Kennedy stronghold of Massachusetts politics (where Jack, his father Joseph, and his younger brother Teddy had made their political careers) showed the strength and resilience of Bobby Kennedy's candidacy and his self-confidence in striving for higher elective office.

When Bobby Kennedy declared his intention to contest the 1968 race, it even unnerved many Democrats who thought that the Kennedy era was over with the assassination of John F. Kennedy. But, Bobby was determined more than ever to carry the Kennedy legacy further. But he wanted to do it his way based on his experience as a U.S. senator representing New York and also his experience being the Attorney General of the United States during both the Kennedy and Johnson presidencies. Jackie wholeheartedly supported Bobby's candidacy.

Jackie was keenly aware of the importance of the primary election and the presidential nominating process, as she herself had been very much involved in the unsuccessful bid made by her husband for the 1956 presidential election and also the 1960 presidential election in which Jack won his party's nomination and eventually the race for the presidency.

At a time when Bobby Kennedy's victory was all but assured with a key victory in the electorally rich state of California, the news of Bobby's assassination by Sirhan Sirhan Bishara completely shattered Jackie. She was in profound shock and seemed to think that there was a malicious conspiracy to eliminate Kennedy's from serving in public life. Upon learning of Bobby Kennedy being shot dead inside a Los Angeles hotel, Jackie said, "I despise America and I don't want my children to live here. If they're killing Kennedy's, my kids are number one targets."[26]

Bobby Kennedy's death occurred in the immediate aftermath of the murder of Civil Rights leader, Dr. Martin Luther King, Jr., in Memphis on April 4, 1968. Jackie was in a melancholy mood at this time. Jackie told Bobby's Press Secretary, Frank Mankiewicz, "The rest of the time, it is often rather silly little men running around in their black suits. But the Catholic Church understands death. I'll tell you who else understands death—the black churches. I remember at the funeral of Martin Luther King. I was looking at those faces and I realized that they know death. They see it all the time, and they are ready for it in the way in which a good Catholic is."[27]

---

[26] Pete Hamill, "A Private Life Defined By Wit, Compassion," *New York Newsday*, May 22, 1994, Also, see Ibid, Spoto, p.260

[27] Cited in Arthur M. Schlesinger, Jr.; *Robert Kennedy and His Times*, Boston; Houghton Mifflin, 1978, p.915

Bobby's assassination was the second consecutive personal tragedy for Jackie. Apart from losing her two pregnancies, she had lost her husband, Jack, under similar tragic circumstances in 1963 in Dallas, Texas. For Jackie, it was time to say 'good bye' to America and look for an alternative place to live her life along with her children.

Chapter 8

BLOSSOMING OF A GREEK ROMANCE: JACKIE'S MARRIAGE TO ARISTOTLE ONASSIS

In 1968, with the assassination of Bobby Kennedy (who was trying to win the Democratic Party presidential nomination) along with the killing of Dr. Martin Luther King, Jr., Jackie was disillusioned with the domestic scene in America and wanted to get away both for her children's safety and to find her inner self and happiness.

Around this time, Jackie secretly was meeting Aristotle Onassis, a Greek shipping magnate and the owner of Olympic Airways. They met at various locations and Ari (as he was called by his friends and relatives) was even introduced to close family members and friends of Jackie as her prospective future suitor. Ari was at this time sixty-two years of age and Jackie was thirty-nine. Before Jackie flew to Greece for the wedding, she went to Boston to seek counsel from Cardinal Cushing of the Catholic Archdiocese of Boston, who had been a family friend of the Kennedy's for a very long time.

CARDINAL'S CONSENT

When he was asked about the state of Jackie's soul, Cardinal Cushing had no patience. "Months ago" said this learned and compassionate pastor:

> "I knew full well that Jacqueline Kennedy was going to marry Aristotle Onassis. I know what she has been going through for many, many months. I have been contacted by many of those who are identified in high places with the administration of the late President Kennedy and I have been contacted by others intimately related and associated with the Kennedy family, to stop all this from taking place – namely that Jack's widow, God rest him, would marry Aristotle Socrates Onassis. Well, I would have no part. Now I turn on the radio and I hear people are knocking her head off, criticizing her and so forth. All I am able to tell you is this. Caritas – Charity? Why do people send so many letters, considering her, considering me? I never would condemn anybody. And this idea of saying she's excommunicated, she's a public sinner – what a lot of nonsense, only God knows who is a sinner, who is not. Why can't she marry whomever she wants to marry? And why

should I be condemned for saying it, and she be condemned for doing it?"[28]

In spite of the Cardinal's misgivings about Jackie's remarriage to a much older man than her, he gave Jackie his blessings and the 'go ahead' from the church to proceed to Greece to marry Onassis. Jackie, along with Senator Edward Kennedy and her children Caroline and John, Jr., as well as some close friends, flew to Athens on October 15, 1968 aboard Olympic Airways from New York's Kennedy International Airport.

As part of the prenuptial agreement, it was decided that Onassis would give Jackie $3 million dollars as a kind of reverse dowry and $1 million for each of her two children. The world press reacted to the news of Jackie's marriage to Aristotle Onassis as a sign of disbelief, and one newspaper described Jackie as a "supertanker" because of the extravagant costs involved in this lavish wedding. The marriage took place on Skorpios Island on October 20 and was attended by family members from both sides.

Although Jackie's marriage to Aristotle Onassis lasted for close to seven years, it was dubbed as a mismatch from the start. After the initial euphoria was over, Ari strongly resented Jackie's lavish lifestyle of buying very expensive clothing. Her shopping sprees in Paris and Monte Carlo cost Ari a substantial fortune.

On top of that, Ari's children, namely daughter Christina and son Alexander, never really warmed up to their step-mother, Jackie, and remained aloof from her during most social and family events and parties.

---

[28] Ibid, Spoto, p.267. Also, see, *The New York Times*, October 24, 1968

As it happened, Ari's fortune in Olympic Airways and his stocks in various companies plummeted deeply, thus making a dent into his vast wealth. Ari's son, Alexander, died in an air crash, which devastated Ari further. Ari attributed it to the 'bad luck' that Jackie brought into his life.

For her part, Jackie found it to be difficult to be away from her children, Caroline and John, Jr., who were studying in the United States. She thus made frequent transatlantic trips during the time she was married to Onassis. Jackie was also advised by Kennedy family members that any future political bid by members of the Kennedy clan were being hampered by Jackie marrying a foreigner, a non-American citizen. Jackie was also very suspicious of Maria Callas, long-time lover of Ari. It turned out that Ari and Maria had continued their romantic liaison even after Ari's marriage to Jackie. Towards the mid-1970s, Ari was in failing health. At the age of sixty-nine, he died of pneumonia on March 15, 1975.

Chapter 9

BACK TO NEW YORK: POST-ONASSIS YEARS

Upon the death of her second husband, Aristotle Onassis, Jackie again felt lonely. The widow spent a little over five years as the wife of the wealthiest man in Greece, Ari, who died on March 15, 1975 at the age of sixty-nine from pneumonia and other ailments.

At the time of Ari's death, Jackie was in New York attending her daughter Caroline's special program that was featured on NBC. Upon learning of Ari's demise, Jackie immediately flew to Greece to attend the funeral ceremony on Skorpios Island, the same place where she married Aristotle Onassis in 1969. In spite of her grief, Jackie supervised the funeral arrangements with Ari's daughter, Christina, and other family members.

Jackie also released a brief statement to the media who were waiting eagerly in which she said: "Aristotle Onassis rescued me at a moment when my life was engulfed with shadows. He meant a lot to me. He brought me into a world where one could find both happiness and love. We lived through many beautiful experiences together which cannot be forgotten and for which I will be eternally grateful."[29]

For the second time again, Jackie felt lonely and vulnerable. Although Aristotle Onassis had a fortune estimated to be over $1 billion, Jackie had signed a "quit clause" under which she was entitled to $250,000 annually and a stipend for her children, Caroline and John, Jr. until their thirty-first birthdays. Through mutual consultation with the lawyers of Jackie and Christina, it was resolved that Jackie should receive a share of $26 million from Ari's properties.

After the funeral and related ceremonies were over in Greece, Jackie tearfully bade farewell to members of Ari's family and flew back to New York to ponder the next phase of her life. Her prime concern was how to raise Caroline and John, Jr. away from the limelight of the prying eyes of the media who were determined to intrude into all aspects of her family's private lives.

A number of Jackie's friends suggested that she join the literary circles of New York City, the country's premier arts and intellectual Mecca. In doing so, Jackie could immerse herself into the activities that she loved ever since her school days at Miss Porter's School.

Finally, on September 18, 1975, Jackie agreed to join Viking Press, a prestigious publishing house in New York City, as a consulting editor for a token salary of $10,000 a year. Prior to the formal acceptance of this assignment at Viking, Jackie had collaborated with her husband (then Senator John F. Kennedy) in writing *Profiles in Courage*, which had earned for Jack Kennedy the

---

[29] Ibid, Spoto, p.288

Pulitzer Prize. At the time the book was written, Jack was under treatment in a hospital bed and Jackie was dutifully taking notes for Jack and offering suggestions. It was Jackie's task to revise the draft accordingly and put it in to her typewriter and report back to Jack again for proof reading.

During her time as the First lady of the White House, Jackie also produced, *The White House: An Historical Guide*. This guide had received wide attention nationwide as it provided a comprehensive look at the mansion of the Chief Executive of the United States for the first time in the nation's history.

At Viking, Jackie was supposedly treated like other staff members as much as possible and worked dutifully. She meticulously looked over every manuscript being submitted and offered constructive comments whenever needed. The first product of her editorial work at the Viking Press was called, *Remember The Leader: Women in America, 1750-1815*, which was full of portraits, diaries, memories and engravings, etc. It also included pictures of life in the early American Republic and the pivotal role women played in shaping and formulating it. Jackie showed keen interest and enthusiasm in going over minute details of the manuscript and in making sure that the finished product provided an objective portrayal of women's lives as they were during America's early years.

Jackie continued in her position at Viking until the end of 1977 when she noticed an opening for the position of Associate Editor at Doubleday. This prestigious publishing house was also based in Manhattan and was located very close to the apartment where she lived. With a salary of $15,000 a year, Jackie began her new assignment in February of 1978 by reporting to her office suite at 245 Park Avenue, a few blocks north of Grand Central Station.

While at Doubleday, Jackie edited a number of books that later became bestsellers. Among those published works were: Jack Bass' *Taming the Storm*, Carl Elliot's *The Cost of Courage, Memoirs Of Martha Graham in Blood Memory, Autobiography of Gelsey Kirkland in Dancing on My Grave*, and others.

Ruth Prawer Jhabvala, a well known screen and play writer and whose novel, *Poet and Dancer*, Jackie edited, commented, "Jackie's empathy was so total...I felt I could lean on her strength which came from her own vulnerability: she was aware how you felt because she felt it herself and knew exactly when and how you needed her support."[30] All along, no matter which manuscript was being submitted to Jackie for scrutiny and worthiness of being publishable or not, Jackie was extremely methodical in her work, taking her job very seriously. She also accepted friendly comments and editorial advice from her superiors at Doubleday and did not hesitate to back off if a better explanation was offered as to the merits of the numerous manuscripts that were submitted to the publishing house each week.

William La Riche, a writer, said of Jackie. "As a trusted friend, Jackie was eager to connect on the deepest possible level, and she had a greater capacity for empathy than anyone else I had ever met. The truth is that she was the most spiritually generous friend I have ever known – a woman with an amazing ability to see into one's life more deeply and usefully than one could imagine. I once asked her, during the most painful moments of her life, how she had the

---

[30] "Informed Sympathy", *A Tribute to Jacqueline Kennedy Onassis*, New York: Doubleday, 1995, p.11

strength to go on, and she replied, 'It never occurred to me not to.'"[31] Jackie's resilience and strong determination won for her wide accolades among her fellow staff members who, at times, were worried that Jackie was perhaps expending too much energy, even at the cost of jeopardizing her frail health and physical well-being.

FOREIGN TRIPS

During the time she spent in New York City working, first for Viking and later for the Doubleday, Jackie also made several foreign trips to fulfil her love for travel and culture.

In May 1978, Jackie made her first journey to Israel for the dedication of the Jewish Diaspora Museum in Tel Aviv. She inquired of the staff about the Ashkenazi and Sephardim Jews who had migrated to Israel historically since the state was created in 1948. In the same trip, Jackie visited biblical sites inside and outside the city of Jerusalem including Bethlehem and planted a tree in the John F. Kennedy Memorial Forest.

In October 1978, Jackie, accompanied by her children, Caroline and John, Jr., attended the dedication ceremony of Harvard University's John F. Kennedy School of Government. Jackie wholeheartedly supported this model think tank that was to develop critical thinking in many vital areas of public policy. The institute was also responsible for providing useful career advice to young and upcoming government officials.

In spite of being busy with a number of activities, Jackie made sure that her children's welfare and overall interest were not being

---

[31] Ibid, Spoto, p.317

neglected. To mark Caroline's twenty-first and John, Jr.'s eighteenth birthdays in November 1978, she brought both of them (John, Jr. was at the Phillips Academy as a Senior waiting for his graduation in June 1979 and Caroline was Junior at the Radcliffe College) to her Manhattan apartment and arranged a disco party for guests at Le Club on East Fifty-Fifth Street.

Jackie celebrated her fiftieth birthday in July 1979 with her close friends, quietly sailing in Nantucket Sound. It also showed Jackie's fascination with and love of the ocean since most of her life was spent on places near the sea, whether it was Long Island, Martha's Vineyard, Hyannisport, or Skorpios Island. Jackie once said, "When I go down by the sandy shore, I can think of nothing I want more than to live by the booming blue sea, as the seagulls flutter round about me."[32]

One of Jackie's close friends, Marianne Velman, who sold British Broadcasting rights for Doubleday from a London office, commented of Jackie's sixteen years with Doubleday in the words:

> "I found her amazingly easy to deal with, approachable and friendly, relaxed and completely professional. She projected no formality or airs—on the contrary, she was entirely natural in everything she did and said, even when we rode in the elevator and she swiftly and casually put on her dark glass and head scarf, the disguise she often wore to preserve her privacy. I found it odd, however, that for many people outside, it was as if this important third part of her life didn't exist. She was usually spoken of and

---

[32] Ibid, Spoto, p.312. Also, note, Jackie's poem was published in *People Magazine*, July 13, 1981.

written about as if she were this character from the
past. But she was very much a person of the
present."[33]

It was to Jackie's credit that she never allowed her celebrity
status to dominate her inner self. Jackie's attention to minute details
in literary works and her single-minded devotion to editorial tasks
both at Viking as well as at Doubleday earned her fulsome praise
from her friends and associates.

---

[33] Ibid, Spoto, p.314-315

Chapter 10

END OF AN AMERICAN ICON

Toward the end of 1993 and in the Spring of 1994, Jackie complained to her friends at Doubleday of constant headaches and a weakening of her body. Jackie had also become prone to colds and other forms of allergies. Although her colleagues at Doubleday Publishing urged Jackie to take a few days off from her hectic schedule in order to recover physically, Jackie stubbornly resisted the idea.

By April of 1994, Jackie was diagnosed as having non-Hodgkin's lymphoma, a life-threatening form of cancer. Although the doctors at the Cornell University Medical Center where she was treated earlier, recommended a bone marrow transplant, Jackie refused to go along with the physician's method of treatment.

Perhaps, Jacqueline Kennedy had a premonition that her end was fast approaching and she wanted to lead her life her own way in those final days. On Sunday, May 15, 1994, Jackie took a walk in Central Park, which was close to her apartment. Her constant companion of later years, Maurice Templesman and her grand children (children of her daughter Caroline and Edward Schlossberg) kept Jackie company in the final months of her life, including the day she strolled through Central Park. Jackie was seen by the Sunday crowd in Central Park that day to be treating the kids to ice cream.

The same evening, Jackie complained of uneasiness and pain and was taken to the hospital. The doctors attending Jackie diagnosed her as suffering from an acute case of pneumonia. The doctors also told Jackie that her cancer cells had already spread to the liver and that she was in a very delicate situation.

Jackie remained in the hospital from May 16 through May 18, when she ultimately voluntarily decided not to go through the painful process of chemotherapy and other related treatment plans. Accordingly, acceding to her request, the hospital authorities discharged Jackie from the cancer unit so that she could go back to her residence at 1040 Park Avenue in Manhattan in order to spend the final moments of her life at home.

By May 18, 1994, almost all of the Kennedy extended family members were near Jackie's bed, including Senator Edward Kennedy of Massachusetts, her daughter Caroline, her son John, Jr., Caroline's husband, Edward Schlossberg, and hosts of cousins and relatives both from her father and mother's sides as well as in-laws. While all of them were praying for a last minute miraculous recovery of Jacqueline Kennedy, reality was dawning upon them that the end was near.

Finally, with her close relatives by her side and a priest who quickly read the last sermon and administered it to her, Jacqueline

Kennedy Onassis breathed her last on Thursday, May 19, 1994, at 10:15 pm.

The next day, her son, John F. Kennedy, Jr., made a simple announcement to the waiting press and the media at large who had gathered in front of her Manhattan apartment. John, Jr. said, "Jackie did it her own way and on her own terms and we all feel lucky for that."[34] Maurice Templesman, Jackie's companion in her later years said, "Jackie went out with her usual courage and style."[35]

The funeral service was held on Monday, May 23, in the church of St. Ignatius Loyola in the presence of scores of dignitaries including President Bill Clinton and First Lady Hillary Rodham Clinton.

EULOGIES

In the memorial service, two of Jackie's favorite poems, "Ithaka" by C.P. Cavafy, and "Merry of Cape Cod" by Edna St. Vincent Milloy were read. The latter was taken out from the prize book which Jackie had earnestly won and was awarded at Miss Porter's School in 1946. It evoked past summers on the Cape, the long beautiful shore line and the blue ocean waters that Jackie loved and in which she shared the best moments of her life with Jack.

> "The wind in the ash-tree sounds like surf on the
> shore of Truro
> I will shut my eyes ……..

[34] Sarah Bradford, *America's Queen: The Life of Jacqueline Kennedy Onassis*, New York: Vikings, 2000, p.440
[35] Ibid, Bradford, p.440

They said: leave your pebbles on the sand, and your
shells
too, and came along
We'll find you another beach like the beach at Truro
Let me listen to the wind in the ash ..... it sounds
Like Surf In the Shore"[36]

Cavafy's "Ithaka" invoked the adventure of Ulysses, which had
played such a pivotal part in Jackie's life during her marriage to
Aristotle Onassis, and which in a way symbolized her spirit of
adventure, as well as her sense of having reached the end of her
journey.

"As you set out for Ithaka
Hope your road is a long one,
Full of adventure, full of discovery
Laistrygonias Cyclops
Angry Poseidon a don't be afraid of them
You'll never find things like that on your way
As long as you keep your thoughts raised high,
As long as a rare experiment
Stirs your spirit and your body.......
Hope your road is a long one,
May there be summer mornings when,
With what pleasure, what joy,
You enter harbors you're seeing for the first time......
Keep Ithaka always in your mind
Arriving there is what you're destined for,
But don't hurry the journey at all.
Better if it lasts for years, so you're old by the time
you

[36] Ibid, Bradford, p. 442

Reach the island
Wealthy with all you've gained along the way
Wise as you will have become, so full of
Experience, you'll have understood by then
What these Ithakans mean......"[37]

Maurice Templesman added his own farewell.

"And now the journey is over
too short, alas, too short
It was filled with
Adventure and wisdom
Laughter and love, gallantry and grace..."[38]

Later, the casket carrying Jackie's coffin was carried by Kennedy family members and flown to Washington D.C., where she was buried next to her husband, the late President John Fitzgerald Kennedy and their son, Patrick, and daughter, Arabella. Thus ended the life of the most famous woman of her times who remained an icon to many people both within America and in the wider world. *The New York Daily News* described Jackie's death with a solemn headline in the front page, that just read "Miss You". Yes, Americans missed Jackie very much. She and Jack provided the most fascinating spectacle in the image of Camelot during the time they lived in the White House. Jackie, on her own, showed the world her extraordinary candor and magnetic personality. She captivated the hearts of many who came in contact with her and

[37] Ibid, Bradford, p. 442-443
[38] Ibid, Bradford, p.443

were touched by her warmth, sense of humor, and taste for delectable artistic perfection. She is still missed by countless people.

BIBLIOGRAPHY

Adler, Bill. *The Kennedy Children: Triumphs and Tragedies*. New York: Franklin Watts, 1980

Adler, Bill, Ed. *The Unknown Wisdom of Jacqueline Kennedy Onassis*. New York: Citadel, 1994

Anderson, Christopher. *Jackie after Jack*. New York; Morrow, 1998

Anthony, Carl Sferrazza. *As We Remember Her*. New York: Harper and Collins, 1997

Baldrige, Letitia. *In the Kennedy Style*. New York: Madison Press/Doubleday, 1998

Birmingham, Stephen. *Jacqueline Bouvier Kennedy Onassis*. New York: Grosset and Dunlop, 1978

Bishop, Jim. *The Day Kennedy Was Shot*. New York: Bantam, 1969

Boller, Paul F. *Presidential Wives*. New York; Oxford University Press, 1988

Bouvier, Jacqueline and Lee Bouvier. *One Special Summer*. New York: Delacorte Press, 1974

Bradlee, Benjamin C. *Conversation With Kennedy*. New York: Norton, 1975

Caroli, Betty Boyd. *First Ladies*. New York; Oxford University Press, 1987

Carpozi, George. *The Hidden Side of Jacqueline Kennedy*. New York: Pyramid Books, 1967

Carpozi, George. *Jackie and Ari: For Love or Money?* New York: Lancer Books, 1968

Cassini, Oleg. *A Thousand Days of Magic: Dressing Jacqueline Kennedy for the White House*. New York: Rizzoli, 1995.

Collier, Peter and David Horowitz. *The Kennedy's: An American Dream*. New York: Summit Books, 1984.

Curran, Robert. *The Kennedy Women: Their Triumphs and Tragedies*. New York: Lancer Books, 1964.

Damore, Leo. *The Cape Cod Years of John Fitzgerald Kennedy*. Englewood Cliffs, N.J. Prentice–Hall, 1967

David, Lester. *Jacqueline Kennedy Onassis: A Portrait of Her Private Years*. New York: Birch Lane/Carol, 1994

Davis, John H. *The Bouviers: Portrait of an American Family*. New York: Farrar, Strauss and Giroux, 1969

Davis, John H. *Jacqueline Bouvier: An Intimate Memoir*. New York: John Wiley, 1996

Davis, John H. *The Kennedy's: Dynasty and Disaster, 1848-1983*. New York: McGraw-Hill, 1984.

Evans, Peter. *Ari: The Life and Times of Aristotle Socrates Onassis*. New York: Summit Books, 1986.

Fraser, Nicholas, et al. *Aristotle Onassis*. Philadelphia: Lippincott, 1977.

Frischauer, Willi. *Onassis*. New York; Meredith Press, 1968.

Galbraith, John Kenneth. *Ambassador's Journal; A Personal Account of the Kennedy Years*. London: Hamish Hamilton, 1969.

Gallagher, Mary Bareli (with Frances Spatz Leighton). *My Life With Jacqueline Kennedy*. New York; David McKay, 1969

Gallella, Ron. *Jacqueline*. New York; Sheed and Ward, 1974

Gutin, Myra G. *The President's Partner: The First Lady in the Twentieth Century*. New York: Greenwood press, 1989

Hall, Gordon Langley and Ann Pinchot. *Jacqueline Kennedy*. New York: Frederick Fell, 1964

Harding, Robert T. *Jacqueline Kennedy: A Woman for the World*. New York; Encyclopedia Enterprises, 1966; distributed by Vanguard Press.

Heller, Deane and David Heller. *Jacqueline Kennedy; The Warmly Human Life Story of the Woman All Americans Have Taken To Their Heart*. Derby, CT: Monarch Books, 1963.

Heymann, C. David. *A Woman Named Jackie: An Intimate Biography of Jacqueline Bouvier Kennedy Onassis*. New York: Lyle Stuart, 1989

Klein, Edward. *Just Jackie*. New York: Ballantine, 1998

Koestenbaum, Wayne. *Jackie Under My Skin: Interpreting an Icon*. New York: Farrar, Strauss and Giroux, 1995

Ladowsky, Ellen. *Jacqueline Kennedy Onassis*. New York; Park Lane Press, 1997

Lawliss, Charles. *Jacqueline Onassis, 1929-1994*. New York: JG Press, 1994

Leamer, Laurence. *The Kennedy Women: The Saga of an American Family*. New York: Villard Press, 1994

Longford, Lord. *Kennedy*. London: Weldenfeld and Nicholson, 1976

Lowe, Jacques. *Jacqueline Kennedy Onassis: The Making of a First Lady*. Los Angeles: General Publishing Group, 1996

Martin, Patricia Miles. *Jacqueline Kennedy Onassis*. New York; G.P.Putnam's Sons, 1955

Martin, Ralph G. *A Hero For Our Times: An Intimate Story of the Kennedy Years*. New York: MacMillan, 1983

Means, Marianne. *The Woman in the White House: The Lives, Times and Influence of Twelve Notable First Ladies*. New York: Random House, 1963

Moutsatsos, Kiki Feroudi with Phyllis Karas. *The Onassis Women*. New York: Putnam's, 1998

Onassis, Jacqueline. "Being Present", *The New Yorker*, January 13, 1975, p.26-28

Osborne, Claire G; ed. *Jackie; A Legend Defined*. New York: Avon Books, 1997

Parmet, Herbert S. Jack: *The Struggles of John F. Kennedy*. New York: Dial, 1980

Reeves, Richard. *President Kennedy: Profile of Power*. New York: Simon and Schuster, 1993

Remembering Jackie- A Life in Pictures. New York: Warren Books, 1994.

Rhea, Mini. *I was Jacqueline Kennedy's Dressmaker*. New York: Fleet, 1962

Salinger, Pierre. *With Kennedy*. Garden City, New York: Doubleday, 1966

Schlesinger, Arthur M; Jr. *A Thousand Days: John F. Kennedy In the White House*. Boston: Houghton Mifflin, 1965

Sidey, Hugh. *John F. Kennedy, President.* New York: Atheneum, 1963

Shulman, Irving. *Jackie! The Exploitation of a First Lady.* New York: Trident Press, 1970

Sorensen, Theodore C. *Kennedy.* New York: Harper and Row, 1965

Suares, J.C. and J. Spencer Beck. *Uncommon Greece's Reminiscences and Photographs of Jacqueline Bouvier Kennedy Onassis.* Charlottesville, Va: Thomasson-Grant, 1994

Thayer, Mary Van Renssalaer. *Jacqueline Bouvier Kennedy.* Garden City, N.Y. Doubleday, 1961

Thomas, Helen. *Dateline White House: A Warm and Revealing Account of America's Presidents and Their families, from the Kennedy's to the Fords.* New York: Macmillan Publishing, 1975

Tribute to Jacqueline Kennedy Onassis, A. New York: Doubleday, 1995

Truman, Margaret. *First Ladies.* New York: Random House, 1995

Watney, Hedda Lyons. *Jackie O.* New York: Leisure Books, 1979

West, J.B. with Mary Lynn Kotz. *Upstairs at the White House: My Life With the First Ladies.* New York: Coward, McCann and Geoghegan, 1973

White, Theodore H. *In Search of History; A Personal Adventure.* New York; Warner Books, 1978

INDEX

A

Adams, Abigail, ix
Addison's disease, 13
advisors, 19, 25, 55
African-Americans, 22
aides, 40, 49
Air Force One, 47
American icon, xi
American public, xiii, 53
American Republic, 67
American society, xi, xv, 30
Andrews Air Force, 44, 47
Arlington National cemetery, 49
art, xii, 19, 32, 40
Arthur, Chester A., viii
Arthur, Ellen, viii
assassination, viii, xiii, 53, 55-59,
61

Attorney General of the United
States, 57
Austria, 38
autopsy, 48

B

Bagh, Shalimar, 41
ballet, 32
Bastille, 6
Bay of Pigs, 37
Beatles, 32
Berlin Wall, 37
Bernstein, Leonard, 32
Bethesda Naval Hospital, 48
Bird, Lynda, 51
Bishara, Sirhan Sirhan, 58
Blue Room, 28
Bouvier II, John, xi
Bouvier, Bud, 1

Bouvier, Jack, 1, 2, 12, 17
brokerage firm, 1
Buchanan, James, viii
Buckingham Palace, 39
burial ceremony, 49
Bush, Barbara, x

C

cabinet officials, 25
California, 58
Callas, Maria, 64
Cambodia, 42, 56
Camelot, xiii, 52, 77
Canada, 38
Canadian Prime Minister, 38
Cape Cod, 4, 21, 25, 75, 80
Capitol Building, 15, 48
Capitol Rotunda, 48
Casals, Pablo, 32
Cassini, Oleg, 30
Catholic, 20, 24, 58, 62
CBS, 22
Central Park, 73
Checker, Chubby, 32
Chief Executive, 47, 67
China, 32, 42
Churchill, Winston, 19
Civil Rights, 23, 58
classical music, 12
Cleveland, Grover, viii, 25
Clinton, First Lady Hillary
   Rodham, 75
Clinton, President Bil, vii l, 75
Cold War, 27

Colorado, California, 33
Columbia, 39
concerts, 32
congressional records, 13
Connally, Governor John, 44, 45,
   48
Connally, Mrs. John, 45
Constitution, ix
Copland, Aaron, 32
Cornell University, xv, 73
Cuban Missile Crisis, 37

D

Dallas Airport, 45
Dallas, Texas, xii, 34, 43, 45, 47,
   48, 53, 55, 59
de Gaulle, Charles, xii, 38
debutante of the year, 5
Democratic Administration, 31
Democratic Party, 16, 19-21, 25,
   44, 53, 61
Democrats, 25, 53, 57
designer fashions, 30
Diefenbaker, John, 38
Doubleday, xiii, 67-71, 73, 79, 82,
   83
Dowds, Jules, 14

E

East Hampton, xi, 2
Eisenhower, Mamie, 26
Eisenhower, President Dwight, 10,
   16, 23, 25

Eisenhower-Nixon, 16
election results, 23
electoral college, 44
electoral votes, 21, 24
England, xii, 6, 19, 33
eternal flame, 49
Executive Mansion, vii, 31

F

family, ix
first ladies, vii, ix, x
Florida, xvii, 14, 25
foreign dignitaries, 28, 32, 49
founding fathers, ix
France, 6, 32, 37, 38
French antiques, 12
French Civilization, 6
French language, 6

G

Galbraith, John Kenneth, 18, 39,
    52
Gandhi, Mohandas K., 40
Gandhi, Mrs. Indira, 40
George Washington University,
    xii
Georgetown, 13, 53, 56
Germany, 33
Gilpatric, Deputy Secretary of
    State Roswell, 37
global dominance, 37
Goa, 39
Governor of Texas, 44

Grand Central Station, 68
grassroots workers, 44
Greece, xiii, 61, 63, 65, 66, 83

H

Harriman, Averall, 53, 56
Harrison, Caroline, viii
Harvard University, 69
Hassan, King, 38
Hawaii, 33
Hill, Clint, 46
historic moments, 37
House of Representatives, 48
Hugh Auchincloss, 3, 4, 6, 12
Humphrey, Hubert, 20
Husted, John, 9, 10
Hyannisport, 12, 23, 24, 70

I

ideological arena, 37
inaugural speech, 28
inauguration, viii
India, xii, xv, 39, 40, 41, 42, 53
India-American relations, 41
Indo-China, 42, 57
interior decoration, 28
international diplomacy, 37
Ireland, 33
Italy, 6, 33

J

Jackson, Andrew, viii

Jackson, Rachel, viii
Jahan, Shah, 41
Jazz, 32
Jefferson, Thomas, viii
Jewel in the Crown, 39
John F. Kennedy Memorial Forest,
    69
John F. Kennedy School of
    Government, 69
Johnson, Lyndon B., (LBJ) xiii,
    21, 33, 43-45, 47, 50, 55

K

Kefauver, Estes, 16
Kennedy clan, 24, 64
Kennedy Doctrine for nuclear
    disarmament, 37
Kennedy International Airport, 63
Kennedy, Caroline Bouvier, viii,
    2, 17, 25, 30, 48-50, 53, 63-66,
    69, 70, 74
Kennedy, Ethel, 53
Kennedy, Joseph (Joe), 11, 19
Kennedy, Jr., John F., 26, 48-50,
    53, 63, 64, 66, 69, 70, 74, 75
Kennedy, Patrick Bouvier, 34, 77
Kennedy, President John
    Fitzgerald (JFK), 24, 47, 48,
    55, 77
Kennedy, Robert (Bobby), 12, 17,
    21, 23, 47, 49, 53, 57-59, 61
Kennedy, Senator Edward
    (Teddy), 49, 63, 74
Kennedy-Johnson, 26, 44

Khan, Field Marshall Ayub, 41
Khruschev, Nikita, xii, 39
Khyber Pass, 41
King, Jr., Dr. Martin Luther, 23,
    58, 61
King, Mrs. Coretta Scott, 23
Korean War, 27

L

Lady Bird, 45, 47, 50, 51
Latin American bossa nova, 32
Lee, Janet, xi, 1
Lee, Jim, 1
Lincoln, Evelyn, 14
literature, xv, 6, 12
London, 10, 19, 39, 70, 81, 82
Long Island, xi, xii, 2, 70

M

Majority Leader, 51
Manhattan, xi, 2, 10, 67, 70, 74,
    75
Martha's Vineyard, 70
Massachusetts, xii, xvii, 6, 9, 11,
    18, 19, 57, 74
media outlets, 26
Morocco, 38

N

Nantucket Sound, 70
NATO, 38
NBC, 65

Nehru, Prime Minister Jawaharlal, 40
New Frontier, 28
New York City, xi, xiii, 1, 12, 17, 18, 56, 66, 69
newspapers, 13, 26, 39
Nixon, Richard, 22-24, 44
Nixon-Cabot Lodge, 44
non-Hodgkin's lymphoma, 73
North African region, 38
Nuclear Test Ban Treaty, 15

O

oath of office, 47
O'Donnell, Kenneth, 46
Olympic Airways, 61, 63, 64
Onassis Aristotle (Ari), xiii, 61-66, 76, 80
Onassis, Christina, 34, 63, 65, 66
Oswald, Lee Harvey, 48
outgoing administration, 26
Oval Office, 25

P

painful ordeal, 53
Pakistan, xii, 39, 41
Paris, xii, 6, 19, 38, 63
Pentagon, 38
personal attendants, 40
photographers, 40
popular vote, 24
Potomac river, 15, 49
Powers, Dave, 46

presidency, vii, ix, x
presidential advisors, ix
presidential election, 16, 17, 33, 39, 57, 58
presidential limousine, 45, 46
presidential motorcade, 45-47
presidential wives, viii, ix
press corps, ix
Profiles in Courage, 14
Puerto Rico, 39
Pulitzer Prize, 15, 67

Q

Queen Elizabeth II, 10, 39
Queen of America, 42

R

Radhakrishnan, President Dr. S., 40
Radziwill, Lee, 3, 10, 34
Radziwill, Stanislas, 19
Red Room, 28
reporters, 40
Republican Administration, 16
restoration, 31
Robertson, Nan, 25
Roosevelt, Eleanor, 21, 26
Roosevelt, Franklin D. , 21, 34
Ruby, Jack, 48

S

S. S. Aquitania, 2

Schlossberg, Edward, 74
Schneider, Alexander, 32
Secret Service Agents, 40
Secret Service, 25, 40, 45, 46, 49
Secretary of State, 37, 53
Senate Majority Leader, 21, 33
Senate, 9, 10, 13-15, 17, 19, 21,
    33, 48, 51
Sihanouk, Prince Norodam, 42, 56
Skorpios Island, xiii, 63, 65, 70
social conventions, viii
Sorbonne, xii, 6, 37, 38
Sorensen, Theodore, 14, 52
Soviet Union, 15, 37
speech writers, 40
sphere of influence, 37
state governors, 48
State of the Union Message, 51
Stern, Isaac, 32
Stevenson, Adlai, 16
Stevenson-Kefauver, 16
swearing in ceremony, 29, 47

T

Taj Mahal, 40
Templesman, Maurice, 74, 75, 77
Texas Book Depository, 45
Texas, 21, 23, 33, 34, 43-45, 51
Thailand, 42
Truman, Margaret (Bess), 26, 27
Truman, President Harry, 27
TV networks, 48
Tyler, John, viii, 25
Tyler, Letitia, viii

U

U.S. Ambassador to India, 39
U.S. Constitution, 47
U.S. flag, 48
U.S. Senator, 33
Under Secretary of Commerce, 34
United Nations, vii

V

Van Buren, Martin, viii, 32
Vassar College, xii, 5
Venezuela, 39
victory parties, 25
Vienna, xii, 39
Vietnam, 15, 42, 57
Viking (Press), xiii, 40, 66, 67, 69,
    71
Virginia, 4, 15, 19, 30
Vogue magazine, 6, 11

W

Wall Street, 1
Warren Commission, 45, 46
Washington Senate, 14
Washington Times-Herald
    newspaper, 7
Washington, D.C., 6, 12, 19, 25,
    29, 30, 34, 44, 49, 53, 56
Washington, Martha, ix
Western India, 39
White House, vii-xii, 18, 23-33,
    48-50, 52, 55, 67, 77, 80, 82, 83

Wilson, Ellen, viii
Wilson, Woodrow, viii
Wisconsin, 19, 20
women, viii, ix, x
World War II, 27

Y

Yale University, 1
Yarborough, Senator Ralph, 43